SIX THINKING HATS® FOR SCHOOLS

K-2 Resource Book

by
Edward de Bono

This series of teacher resource books represents the only authorized
educational adaptation of the six hats method. This material
is written and designed by the originator of the six hats
method, Edward de Bono, specifically for use in education.

Consultants:

Lori J. Alexander
Third Grade Teacher
Western Hills Elementary School
West Des Moines, Iowa

Pat Antonopoulos
Kindergarten Teacher
Westwood View Elementary School
Shawnee Mission, Kansas

Cathy Battaglia
Staff Development Specialist
Niagara Falls City School District
Niagara Falls, New York

Christine Bialik
First Grade Teacher
Hyde Park School
Niagara Falls, New York

Margaret Bielanin
Kindergarten Teacher
Hyde Park School
Niagara Falls, New York

Bonnie DeRosa
First Grade Teacher
Hyde Park School
Niagara Falls, New York

Charleen Gallo
First Grade Teacher
Hyde Park School
Niagara Falls, New York

Martha Hayes
Educational Consultant
Mt. Pleasant, Iowa

Connie Healy
Second Grade Teacher
Stilwell Elementary School
Stilwell, Kansas

Catherine A. House
Gifted and Talented Teacher/Coordinator
Wilson Central Schools
Wilson, New York

Luann Johnson
Kindergarten Teacher
Crestview Elementary School
West Des Moines, Iowa

Deborah Kumm
Second/Third Grade Teacher
Hyde Park School
Niagara Falls, New York

Suzanne Larrabee
First Grade Teacher
Hyde Park School
Niagara Falls, New York

Linda Legg
Kindergarten Teacher
Hyde Park School
Niagara Falls, New York

Patricia Mackenna
First Grade Teacher
Hyde Park School
Niagara Falls, New York

Deborah Pedersen
Educational Consultant
Dunlap, Illinois

Carolyn S. Sharp
First Grade Teacher
Indian Creek Elementary School
Olathe, Kansas

Kathleen Wright
Second Grade Teacher
Hyde Park School
Niagara Falls, New York

Pam Tansy
Program Coordinator
West Des Moines Community Schools
West Des Moines, Iowa

Editor-in-Chief: Kathleen Myers
Managing Editor: Beth Obermiller
Editor: Mary Lindeen
Cover and Book Design: Barbara Gordon
Photography: Craig Anderson
Illustration: Don Tate

ISBN 1-56312-096-8

Published by Perfection Learning Corporation
Copyright 1991. The McQuaig Group Inc.
Printed in U.S.A.

"If we put the factory at that place, then if there is an accident, toxic chemicals will flow into the town's water supply."

"If you go to work in the kitchen with that thumb infection, you could make a lot of people ill with food poisoning."

"If you drop out of school, you will find it harder to get a job for the rest of your life."

We need to be careful to avoid doing things that might do harm to the environment, to others, or to ourselves. What sort of thinking protects us from making such mistakes? This is black hat thinking.

Obviously, black hat thinking is a very important part of thinking. In fact, you could say that black hat thinking may be the most important type of thinking. Certainly the black hat is the most used hat.

I make this point because some people have got the idea that somehow the black hat is not as useful as the other hats. This is an incorrect view based on two mistakes.

1. Because black hat thinking is often used to point out bad things does not mean it is bad thinking.

2. Because overuse and abuse of the black hat may limit thinking does not mean that the black hat as such is a bad hat. Eating too much may make you ill, but this does not mean that food is bad. Drinking too much alcohol may make you an alcoholic, but this does not mean that beer and wine are themselves bad.

This is an important point because all six thinking hats are valuable types of thinking. To consider any one hat as inferior to the others destroys the usefulness of the system.

Without the black hat, we would get into a lot of trouble and cause a lot of harm.

TABLE OF CONTENTS

ABOUT THE AUTHOR

Simple methods used effectively are more valuable than complicated methods that are difficult to understand.

Edward de Bono is a pioneer in the field of the teaching of thinking in education. He first wrote the CoRT program in 1972. This program is now the most widely used program throughout the world for the direct teaching of thinking as a curriculum subject. It is used in the USA, China, USSR, Venezuela, United Kingdom, Singapore, Malaysia, Australia, New Zealand, and in many other countries. This widespread use of Dr. de Bono's

material across different nationalities and cultures is due to the simplicity and robustness of the material. The material can be used by teachers with widely differing backgrounds and qualifications.

Dr. de Bono was a Rhodes scholar at Oxford University and has held faculty appointments at the universities of Oxford, Cambridge, London, and Harvard. He has written thirty books in the general area of thinking. There are translations into twenty-three languages including Japanese, Hebrew, Finnish, Russian, and Urdu.

What is unusual about Dr. de Bono is that he works in the field of education and also for business and government organizations. He has worked with such corporations as IBM, DuPont, Hoechst-Celanese, and many others.

The Six Thinking Hats method is based on Dr. de Bono's very extensive experience in the field of the direct teaching of thinking across different ages and abilities, ranging from six-year-olds to senior corporate executives. It is Dr. de Bono's belief that simple methods used effectively are more valuable than complicated methods that are difficult to understand and confusing to use.

This book is one of a series of resource books for the teaching of the six thinking hats method in schools. The series includes a book for each of these levels: grades K-2, 3-5, 6-8, 9-12, and adult educators. The use of the method is valid at all ages. The teaching of the method will, however, vary with age and ability.

With younger students, the use of each hat can be much simplified. With older and more able students, the use of each hat is more comprehensive and more precise. Simpler exercises are chosen for younger students. There are more difficult exercises provided in the upper-level books.

Time and Place

In some schools, there is a specific allocation of time to the direct teaching of thinking skills. In such cases, the six hats method can be taught directly as part of the thinking skills program.

In schools where there is as yet no provision for the direct teaching of thinking skills, the six hats method can be taught as part of other subject areas. For example, there is always a close link between language and thinking. Language is there to express thinking. If the thinking is poor, then language skills by themselves will not be much use. So the six hats method could be taught as part of language arts.

The six hats framework is also valuable for writing about or talking about any subject. Therefore, the method may be taught as part of such subject areas as reading, social studies, science, or math.

My experience suggests that thinking skills are most effectively taught if they are taught directly and deliberately. So I recommend the direct teaching of the six hats method—with subsequent infusion into other areas. Where this is not practical, then the method can be taught as part of some existing curriculum area—like language.

Thinking skills are most effectively taught if they are taught directly and deliberately.

hen we attempt practical thinking, there are three fundamental difficulties:

1. *Emotions.* We often have a tendency not to think at all but to rely on instant gut feeling, emotion, and prejudice as a basis for action.

2. *Helplessness.* We may react with feelings of inadequacy: "I don't know how to think about this. I don't know what to do next."

3. *Confusion.* We try to keep everything in mind at once, with a mess as a result.

The six thinking hats method is a simple and practical way of overcoming all three difficulties.

Emotions are an important part of thinking and, in the end, all decisions and choices are made on the basis of our feelings. Emotions at the right place in thinking are essential. Emotions at the wrong place can be disastrous. The six hats method allows us to use emotions and feelings at the right place.

Helplessness arises when we do not have any general-purpose thinking actions that can be taken. The six hats method provides us with a basic framework for thinking actions. There are now definite "next steps" that can be taken.

Confusion arises when we try to do too much at once. Often when we try to think about something, our minds go off in several different directions at the same time. The six hats method allows us to take one direction at a time.

Full-Color Thinking, One Color at a Time

In the kitchen, have you ever found yourself stirring a sauce, chopping up carrots, mixing a batter, and reading a recipe all at the same time?

In the classroom, have you ever found yourself taking attendance, collecting milk or lunch money, making announcements, and tending an ill child all at the same time?

We frequently do this sort of thing with our thinking too. We have to keep the information in mind while also trying to be logical and to make sure others are logical. Our

THE SIX THINKING HATS CONCEPT

Thinking is divided into six different modes.

emotions are there all the time too. And we need to be constructive. Occasionally, we might even try to be creative and to produce a new idea. As a result, there is a lot going on all at once.

In full-color printing, the basic colors are printed separately. But in the end, all the colors add up to give full-color printing.

In projection television, we can see that there are three beams, each of which is projecting a different base color. These three colors come together on the screen to give full-color television.

The six hats method does exactly the same for thinking. Instead of trying to do everything at once, we can learn to handle the different aspects of thinking one at a time. In the end, these different aspects come together to give full-color thinking.

Six Colors, Six Hats

In the six hats method, thinking is divided into six different modes, each of which is represented by a different color hat. A brief description of each mode is given here. A full description for each will be provided later.

 Red Hat. Emotions. Intuition, feelings, and hunches. No need to justify the feelings. How do I feel about this right now?

 Yellow Hat. Good points. Why is this worth doing? How will it help us? Why can it be done? Why will it work?

 Black Hat. Bad points. Caution. Judgment. Assessment. Is this true? Will it work? What are the weaknesses? What is wrong with it?

 Green Hat. Creativity. Different ideas. New ideas. Suggestions and proposals. What are some possible ways to work this out? What are some other ways to solve the problem?

White Hat. Information. Questions. What information do we have? What information do we need to get?

 Blue Hat. Organization of thinking. Thinking about thinking. What have we done so far? What do we do next?

It is possible to suggest many further hats for different aspects of thinking. However, I believe that the six hats are enough. More hats would be cumbersome and confusing. Fewer would be inadequate.

Hats and Role-playing

Why hats? There is a traditional association between thinking and hats.

"Put on your thinking cap."

"Let's put on our thinking hats here."

A hat is very simple to put on and to take off. No other piece of clothing can be put on or taken off so quickly and easily. This is relevant because we must be able to put on or take off the different colored hats with ease.

Also, hats often indicate a role. Soldiers can wear special helmets. The police may wear hats to indicate their role. In some countries, judges wear special hats. So as we put on a thinking hat, we take on the role indicated by that particular hat.

Switching Roles

It is very important that every thinker must be able to switch roles: put hats on, take hats off. The hats are not meant to put people into categories. It is totally wrong to say, "She's a green hat thinker" or "He only uses the red hat." Although these may be accurate assessments, if we start to use the hats as categories, then people only want to use the thinking associated with a particular category: ''I am a black hat thinker.'' This is exactly the opposite of the purpose and value of the six hats method, which is to get children and adults to use all six modes of thinking.

Detaching the Ego

One of the great limiting factors in thinking is that our egos are much too involved in our thinking. Our egos get attached to an idea or an argument. We cannot stand back in order to be objective. The role-playing of the six hats method allows the ego to be detached from the thinking.

> ''This is not me but my black hat (yellow, green, etc.) speaking.''

It is in this way that the six hats method takes the ego out of thinking.

Getting Beyond Argument

Normally, if we think an idea is not workable, we will spend all our time arguing against it. With the six hats method, we can learn to put on the yellow hat. In doing so, we now show that, even though the idea seems useless, some good may be found in it.

Instead of saying, ''This is what I think and I know I am right,'' we can learn to say, ''If you want me to play the yellow hat role, I can do that very well.''

We develop a pride in the skill of carrying out the different thinking roles. As a result, our thinking about any matter is more comprehensive and more objective.

With the six hats method, if we do not like a suggestion, we know that there will always be a chance to criticize that idea with the black hat and to express feeling with the red hat. Meanwhile, it is possible to explore the idea with white, yellow, and green hats as well.

Four Uses of the Hats in the Classroom

1. **Put the hat on.** We can ask a child in a discussion to put on a particular color hat. Or we can ask a whole group to use a particular color hat for a few minutes.

   > "I want you to give me some black hat thinking on this idea. What could go wrong if we try this idea out?"

   > "We're stuck. Can you put on your green hat and give us some new ideas about this problem?"

   > "What do we know about this? What are the facts? Give us your white hat thinking."

2. **Take the hat off.** We can ask a child, or a group, to take off a particular color of hat. The children have not consciously put on a hat but seem to be using one. Here we are implying that the thinking that is taking place is of a certain type. We are asking the children to move away from that type of thinking. The six hats system provides a convenient method for this.

   > "That's red hat thinking. Can you take off your red hat for a moment?"

   > "You have given us good black hat thinking. Now please take off your black hat."

   > "You've thought of lots of new ideas, but I think we should take off our green hats now."

3. **Switch hats.** Once children understand the six hats, we can ask for an instant switch in thinking. We can accomplish this by suggesting that a child take off one hat and put on another. This way we can call for a switch in thinking without hurting the child's feelings. We are

not attacking the thinking that is taking place but asking for a change.

> "We've heard the good things. Now let's switch from the yellow hat to the black hat. What might be some problems if we do it this way?"

> "With your black hat, you've done a good job of telling why this idea might not work. Now let's switch to the green hat to see if we can figure out ways to make the idea work."

> "That's an interesting idea. Now let's take off our green hats and put on our white hats. For now, let's talk only about the facts we know."

4. **Signal your thinking.** We can name a hat to show the type of thinking that we are going to use. Use the hats yourself—and point out that you are using them—as you teach the hats to the class.

> "Putting on my black hat, I'm thinking that it won't work to get out the musical instruments now because we won't have enough time to put them away before lunch."

> "Putting on my red hat for a moment, I have to say that I just do not like the idea of using those shelves for the math books. I'm not sure why I don't like that idea."

> "Putting on my green hat, I want to tell you a new idea I thought of for those of you who are working on the computer today. It is only a suggestion."

In summary, we can ask children to put on, take off, switch, or signal hats. We can also put on or take off a hat ourselves. The formality and "game" aspect of the method is one of its greatest virtues. People learn to play the game.

Single Hat and Sequence Use

The hats can be used singly at any point in thinking. In general, this is the major use. The hats are used as a convenience for directing thinking and for switching thinking.

Simple sequences of two or three hats may be used together for a particular purpose. For example, the yellow hat followed by the black hat may be used to assess an idea. The black hat followed by the green hat may be used to improve a design (point out the faults and overcome them).

The Unique Blue Hat

The blue hat is different from the other hats because it is involved with directing the thinking process itself. We are actually using the blue hat whenever we suggest the next hat to be used. The blue hat need not be acknowledged at every turn. It can become awkward to say, for instance, ''Putting on my blue hat, I feel we should have some black hat thinking.''

However, there are some points at which it is often helpful to mention the blue hat. Three such points are at the outset of a discussion, to describe a thinking plan; at midpoint, to restate the thinking goals; and at the end, to summarize what thinking has been done.

''Putting on our blue hats, let's decide what we want to think about and which hats we'll need to use.''

''This is interesting, but I think we are getting away from what we wanted to talk about. Let's wear our blue hats and have someone recall what we decided to talk about today.''

''I want you to put on your blue hat and think of a sentence that tells about what we have been doing today.''

Use of the blue hat need not be confined to talking about the other hats. Any thinking steps at all can be suggested.

Six Hats for Richer Thinking

The six hats method allows children to think more richly and more comprehensively. If we simply ask children to think about something, they are often at a loss. But if they are invited to explore the subject using the framework of the hats, their perceptual powers are quickly expanded. For example, compare the responses given when children are asked to think about the following poem.

Read the poem and tell what you think about it.

I'm Glad the Sky Is Painted Blue

I'm glad the sky is painted blue,
    And the earth is painted green,
With such a lot of nice fresh air
    All sandwiched in between.

—Anonymous

Unassisted
response: "I really like this poem."

"I think it's a very good poem."

Six Hats
response: **Red hat (feelings)**

"I really like this poem."

"This poem makes me feel happy."

White hat (facts)

"This poem is called 'I'm Glad the Sky Is Painted Blue.' "

"We don't know who wrote it."

"It has rhyming words in it."

"It is about the earth."

"It is about fresh air."

Yellow hat (good points)

"This poem reminds people that fresh air is nice."

"This poem gives me a good picture of a paintbrush that would be big enough to paint the sky and the earth."

"It is interesting to think about the earth and sky like they are a great big sandwich."

(Discussion could be continued with the black and green hats.)

The elaboration in the second example shows how the six hats method can expand children's perception. The hats supply cues but allow for open-ended responses. With the hats, children are able to become more self-directed but without aimless drifting. The next section will focus specifically on teaching and using the six hats.

It is not necessary for children to be able to read and write in order to learn to use the six thinking hats, although many of the activities described on the following pages are designed with readers and writers in mind. Lessons can be altered to enable children to respond orally or with drawings, or the teacher can record children's comments on the chalkboard or on chart paper.

There are, however, some skills and concepts that must be mastered before children can successfully use the six thinking hats. The following instructional recommendations were designed with these beginners in mind.

- Without directly mentioning the thinking hats, ask children questions using "hats language." This will help children begin to sort their thoughts and comments into different categories. It will also acquaint them with the hats vocabulary (good points, bad points, facts, new ideas, and so forth). Then when direct instruction takes place, the words and phrases associated with this method will be familiar to them. Here are some examples of hat questions for young children.

"How did you like our field trip?"
(red hat)

"Tell me some facts about fire trucks."
(white hat)

"What are some good things about knowing how to read?"
(yellow hat)

"What might go wrong if we tie the jump rope to the top of the jungle gym?"
(black hat)

"Who has some new ideas for ways the King's men could have put Humpty Dumpty together again?"
(green hat)

19

"What is the first thing we should do when we start our art project? Then what should we do?"
(blue hat)

- Frequently record children's responses to hat questions on large sheets of chart paper. Use markers that match the hat color of the question being asked or write on matching colored paper. (White chalk or a white crayon can be used on dark blue and black paper.) For example, using a blue marker to write instructions for art projects will help children begin to associate the color blue with organization.

- Help children learn the difference between a question and a statement. There are many opportunities during the day to point out examples of questions and statements. An ideal time for reinforcing this distinction is during show-and-tell, when many questions are answered by statements.

- In order for children to understand the distinction between the white hat and the red hat, help them recognize the difference between a fact and an opinion. Point out several examples of fact and opinion as you talk with them during class discussions. Ask children for fact and opinion statements about poems or stories you have shared with them. Sorting fact from opinion often helps clarify classroom conflicts, making this skill valuable for classroom management as well.

- Continue to reinforce color identification skills since these are central to successful use of the six thinking hats.

When children have mastered the skills and concepts of the readiness level, you can move on to direct instruction in the use of the six thinking hats.

To introduce the concept of using hats for thinking, bring in a collection of different kinds of hats, such as a chef's hat, fire fighter's hat, wedding veil, tennis visor, stocking cap, sombrero, and so forth. If this is not possible, bring in pictures of people wearing different hats or make some hats out of construction paper. Invite children to try on the different hats. As they put on each hat, ask them what they might be doing and thinking about while wearing that hat. For example, a fire fighter might be riding in a fire truck, thinking about how to put out the fire and rescue the victims.

Then ask children if they have ever heard of *thinking caps.* Allow them to share their experiences. Tell children that in the coming weeks, they will be learning how to use some special thinking caps or hats. Have on hand real or paper hats in each of the six thinking hats colors. Show these hats to the children, and display them again later when you introduce each hat. Hat patterns are provided on pages 102 and 103.

After discussing the idea of hats in general, help children complete the activity shown on page 22. This activity gives an overview of the six thinking hats. Discussion notes for this activity are on page 23.

Each hat is discussed in more depth in separate lessons beginning with the black hat on page 25. These lessons are designed to teach students one hat per week for six consecutive weeks. Each lesson includes several suggestions for using the hat in a variety of activities throughout the week.

Which Hat?

Directions

Three children are using their thinking hats to talk about having a Ferris wheel on the school playground.

Draw a line from each hat to the child who is using that kind of thinking.

Then color the hats. Look for the color words on each hat.

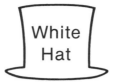

White Hat

Looking for Facts

Yellow Hat

Good Points

Red Hat

Feelings

Matt:
I love Ferris wheels!

Lucy:
It would cool us off on hot days.

Nate:
Would we have to pay for the rides?

Directions

Now three more children tell what they think about the Ferris wheel.

Draw a line from each hat to the child who is using that kind of thinking.

Then color the hats. Look for the color words on each hat.

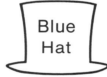

Blue Hat

Thinking About Thinking

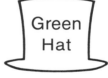

Green Hat

New Ideas

Black Hat

Bad Points

Dave:
Someone might fall off and get hurt.

Dawn:
Let's give extra rides to kids who get all their schoolwork done.

Linn:
Let's make a plan for thinking about this. Maybe we could talk about all the good points first and then all the bad points.

Edward de Bono / Six Thinking Hats for Schools / K-2 Resource Book
Copyright 1991. McQuaig Group / Published by Perfection Learning Corporation

Which Hat? · Teacher Page

Teacher comments for the white hat: The white hat is for getting the facts. Which child wanted more facts about the Ferris wheel? **Nate** asked if the children would have to pay for their rides. Nate wants to know a fact. Draw a line from the white hat to Nate.

Teacher comments for the yellow hat: The yellow hat is for finding good points or telling why something might work. Which child found a good point about having a Ferris wheel? **Lucy** said that the Ferris wheel would cool the children off on hot days. That is a good point. Draw a line from the yellow hat to Lucy.

Teacher comments for the red hat: The red hat is for telling how we feel. Which child told how he or she felt about having a Ferris wheel at school? **Matt** said that he would love it. *Love* is a feeling. Draw a line from the red hat to Matt.

Teacher comments for the blue hat: The blue hat is for thinking about thinking. The blue hat makes a thinking plan. Which child thought about thinking? **Linn** wanted to make a plan to think about the Ferris wheel. Draw a line from the blue hat to Linn.

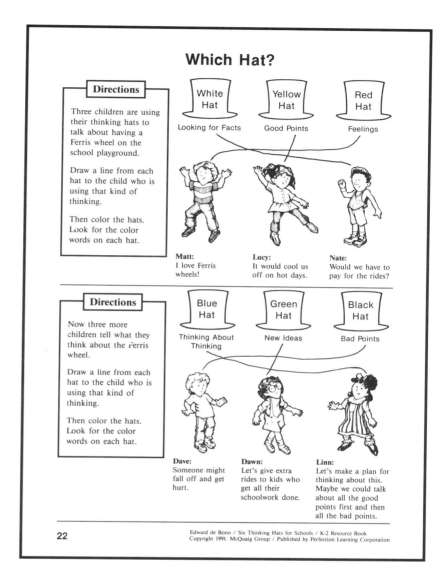

Which Hat?

Directions

Three children are using their thinking hats to talk about having a Ferris wheel on the school playground.

Draw a line from each hat to the child who is using that kind of thinking.

Then color the hats. Look for the color words on each hat.

White Hat — Looking for Facts

Yellow Hat — Good Points

Red Hat — Feelings

Matt: I love Ferris wheels!

Lucy: It would cool us off on hot days.

Nate: Would we have to pay for the rides?

Directions

Now three more children tell what they think about the Ferris wheel.

Draw a line from each hat to the child who is using that kind of thinking.

Then color the hats. Look for the color words on each hat.

Blue Hat — Thinking About Thinking

Green Hat — New Ideas

Black Hat — Bad Points

Dave: Someone might fall off and get hurt.

Dawn: Let's give extra rides to kids who get all their schoolwork done.

Linn: Let's make a plan for thinking about this. Maybe we could talk about all the good points first and then all the bad points.

22

Edward de Bono / Six Thinking Hats for Schools / K-2 Resource Book
Copyright 1991. McQuaig Group / Published by Perfection Learning Corporation

Teacher comments for the green hat: The green hat is for thinking of new ideas or giving suggestions. Which child thought of a new idea? **Dawn** suggested that the children could earn extra rides for getting their schoolwork done. That is a new idea. Draw a line from the green hat to Dawn.

Teacher comments for the black hat: The black hat is for thinking of the bad points or why something won't work. Which child found a bad point about having a Ferris wheel? **Dave** said that someone might fall off of the Ferris wheel and get hurt. That's a bad point. Draw a line from the black hat to Dave.

After working through the **Which Hat?** overview, explain to the children that they can use the six thinking hats to think better about anything. Point out that they will be trying on the hats one at a time in the next few weeks to learn more about each hat.

Summary

When the overview session is finished, invite children to help you list what is now known about the six thinking hats. The main points are summarized below.

If possible, keep the overview session separate and on its own. If, however, time remains which must be used, then go on to the black hat.

Six Hats Color Code

 Red hat: Feelings

 Yellow hat: Good points

 Black hat: Bad points

 Green hat: New ideas

 White hat: Facts

 Blue hat: Thinking about thinking

Six Hats Facts

There are six different colored hats.

Each hat stands for one kind of thinking.

The first hat to be introduced is the black hat. The black hat is for critical thinking. The word *critical* originally comes from the Greek word for judge (*kritikos*). In many countries, judges in court wear black robes because this is a serious color. You may wish to point out to children that wearing the black hat is a serious job.

It is totally wrong to view black hat thinking as bad or undesirable thinking. Using the black hat protects us from making dangerous or unworkable decisions. With the black hat, we find weaknesses and flaws, and we predict problems that may arise. The black hat is perhaps the most often used and the most valuable of all the hats.

The black hat is discussed in more detail in the following teacher notes. Activities for teaching the black hat begin on page 28.

*What is wrong
with this?*

TEACHER NOTES · Black Hat

The following description is intended to serve as background for teacher reference. Consult it when needed to clarify how the black hat may be used and overused.

With the black hat, the words *checking* and *checking out* are very important to explaining its uses. These words convey the essence of critical thinking—and do not carry a negative image.

We know the positive uses of checking something:

In the United States when a new drug is presented by a pharmaceutical company, it is thoroughly checked out by the government's Food and Drug Administration to see that it is not harmful.

In the production and serving of food, there are strict rules of hygiene to prevent the people who eat the food from becoming ill. Inspectors are always checking to see that these rules are followed.

When a manufacturer produces a new toy, this has to be thoroughly checked to be sure that it is not harmful—no sharp edges that might cut, no pieces that might be bitten off and swallowed by a child, etc.

The black hat checks things in the same way. Black hat thinking helps us avoid making mistakes and doing silly things. It also points out difficulties and dangers.

Uses of the Black Hat

The main uses of the black hat are these:

1. Checking for evidence
2. Checking for logic
3. Checking for feasibility
4. Checking for impact
5. Checking for fit
6. Checking for weaknesses

We shall examine each of these uses one after the other. As we do, notice that the purpose of the black hat is not to *attack* but to *examine* an idea or situation.

Checking for Evidence

One use of the black hat is to check the evidence which supports the truth of some statement or claim: Is this true? Is this right? Is this correct? What is the evidence that supports this idea?

Checking for Logic

Another use of the black hat is to check the truth or validity of a logical argument: Does this really follow? Someone may claim that if we have *A* and *B,* then *C* must follow. Black hat thinking checks this claim. We might even check the use of the word *must.* It is possible that *C* might follow, but that is not the same as *must* follow. This is a black hat check for logic.

Checking for Feasibility

With the black hat, we may examine a suggestion to see if it is feasible, possible, or likely to work as claimed. Will this invention work? In practice, can this be done? Will this plan succeed?

With questions like these, we may find actual mistakes or gaps or find that something is missing. For example, a faculty committee that is proposing to implement a new kind of student assessment looks to see if its plan is feasible or workable. The black hat asks if this can be done. How will it work? What might be the difficulties?

Checking for Impact

Anything we do has consequences. Our actions affect other people and the world around us. So we need to get input on the impact of the change before making a final decision.

With the black hat, we may check to see what negative effects a suggestion or idea will have. What might be the difficulties? What dangers are likely to arise? How will this affect other people? How will it affect the environment?

The most important part of checking the impact of an idea is the effect it may have on values. Obviously, the idea suits the values of whoever is making the suggestion—but how does the idea affect others' values?

We need to check the impact of a suggestion very carefully. It may be too late to go back after the idea has been put into use.

Checking for Fit

With the black hat, we may check the fit of what is suggested with what we already know. On a very simple level, we might ask, do these clothes fit? Will this fit in the box? Does the plug fit in the socket?

We also may check an idea to see if it fits the facts as we know them. How does this fit our information? Does this idea fit our experience in this field? Does this fit personal or general experience?

We may also want to know whether an item, policy, or plan fits in with a system: Does this fit the rules, the laws, or the regulations? Does this fit the normal procedures? Does this fit our strategies and objectives?

We can check to see if an idea fits our standards and ethics. Does this plan, policy, or item fit the standards and ethics of our group or society—even if this is not a matter of law? Is this fair? Is this honest?

As for values, we could ask, does this fit our values or the values of our group or society? Here we are not talking about what impact the idea will have on values,

TEACHER NOTES · Black Hat

but whether it fits the existing values.

At the end of this assessment, we could say that something fits, does not fit very well, or does not fit at all.

In practice, there is a big difference between looking at an idea in order to attack or reject it and looking at an idea in order to improve it.

Checking for Weaknesses

Suppose we are presented with a design for a new chair. We look for the weaknesses in the design: the seat is too small, the back is too straight, etc. Our intention may be to reject the design because of these weaknesses.

But our intention may also be to improve the design by pointing out the weaknesses so that they can be overcome. This is a constructive function of the black hat. We search for and point out weaknesses in an idea in order to overcome them, thereby making the idea stronger. When the black hat is used this way, it is generally followed by a green hat search for ways to overcome the weaknesses. This sequence is often called *constructive criticism.*

In practice, there is a big difference between looking at an idea

in order to attack or reject it and looking at an idea in order to improve it.

Questions we might ask to check for weaknesses include these: What are the weaknesses here? What are the weak points in the idea? The word *faults* could be used instead of *weaknesses,* but *weakness* seems a more positive word. A weakness may be minor whereas a fault always seems major and perhaps not correctable.

In summary, the uses of the black hat include checking for evidence, logic, feasibility, impact, fit, and weaknesses. Different mental processes go into these various operations. For example, checking for logical truth means applying the rules of logic. Checking for feasibility may mean applying the rules of engineering or experience of human behavior. Checking for impact involves running something forward in our minds and watching the effects.

Purposes for Using the Black Hat

The two main purposes for using the black hat are to

1. Find weaknesses

2. Make assessments

We may use the black hat early on in our exploration of an idea in order to find the weaknesses. We find these weaknesses in order to overcome them and put them right. When using the black hat to find weaknesses, our goal is to improve upon the idea.

We may use the black hat at the end of an exploration to make an assessment or judgment. When we want to decide on the value of an idea or when we are about to put an idea into action, then we need the black hat to be sure we are not making a mistake. In this final

assessment, we can also follow the black hat with the red hat. After our judgment, how do we now feel about the idea?

Overuse

The black hat is a valuable hat—possibly the most valuable of all—but it can be overused. There are people who only want to use the black hat. They only want to criticize ideas. They feel that this is enough. But it is not.

We need critical thinking, but we also need thinking that is creative, generative, and productive. Where are the ideas and suggestions going to come from? Criticizing ideas may improve them but does not produce new ideas. That is why the teaching of critical thinking by itself is insufficient.

Critical thinking and the black hat have a very important role to play in thinking, but by themselves they are not enough. This is not meant as a rejection of critical thinking but an observation that other kinds of thinking are also needed. One particular wheel on a car may be a very fine wheel, but one wheel alone is not enough to carry the car.

Summary of the Black Hat

The key words to describe the uses of the black hat are *checking* and *checking out.* We can check for evidence, logic, feasibility, impact, fit, and weaknesses. The two main purposes for using the black hat are finding weaknesses and making assessments. The overall question to ask is *What is wrong with this?*

Follow these steps to introduce the black hat: lead-in, explanation, and practice.

Lead-in

Help children recall the overview lesson. Invite them to share what they can remember about the six thinking hats. Explain that they will now have a chance to learn more about one of the hats. Do not identify the color of this hat until after the lead-in. This will give children a chance to guess the hat themselves.

Show children examples of things that have something wrong with them. Give examples with mistakes that children will recognize. At least at first, the errors must be obvious. Following are sample errors.

$$1 + 1 = 9$$

A B C Z E F G

In all cases, ask, "What is wrong with this?" After the easy examples, offer some harder ones. Children should begin to exert an effort to find out what is wrong. It is this effort that is important for black hat use. Mistakes are not always obvious.

Older children may be able to create their own examples of things that have weaknesses or errors. Invite them to do so, then have them trade items and discover what is wrong.

Explanation

After the lead-in, ask children which hat they have been using. If necessary, review all of the hats so that they can remember the choices. Point out that black hat thinking finds reasons why something is bad or wrong or won't work. As you model the use of the black hat, identify specific weaknesses in the topics you're discussing.

> "Putting on my black hat, I'm thinking that if we put those blocks in that box, they will break out of the bottom because they are too heavy."

> "Here's a black hat idea about keeping your lunch ticket in your pocket. You might forget that it's there and take it home. Then you won't have it at school the next day."

Practice

After the lead-in or on another day, have children work individually, in small groups, or as a class to complete the following **Put On Your Black Thinking Hat** reproducible. Read the description and directions aloud, and then invite children to put on their black hats to think about what is wrong with the soda pop drinking fountain.

As children share their responses, write their comments on a large sheet of chart paper using a black marker or a sheet of black paper using a white crayon or white chalk. Post the completed chart in the classroom as a visual reminder of the kind of thinking represented by the black hat.

Consider having children wear black paper hats or visors as you discuss this thinking hat. Hat patterns are provided on pages 102 and 103.

Put On Your Black Thinking Hat

Directions

Here is a school drinking fountain that serves soda pop instead of water. Put on your black hat and think about the bad points of this kind of drinking fountain.

Write the bad points in the space below or share your ideas with the class.

Remember, when you wear your black hat, you are looking for what is **wrong** with something.

Edward de Bono / Six Thinking Hats for Schools / K-2 Resource Book
Copyright 1991. McQuaig Group / Published by Perfection Learning Corporation

Put On Your Black Thinking Hat - Teacher Page

Put On Your Black Thinking Hat

Directions

Here is a school drinking fountain that serves soda pop instead of water. Put on your black hat and think about the bad points of this kind of drinking fountain.

Write the bad points in the space below or share your ideas with the class.

Remember, when you wear your black hat, you are looking for what is **wrong** with something.

Sample black hat comments:

The fountain may not have the kind of soda pop kids like.

The sugar in the soda pop is not good for people's teeth.

The fountains would become sticky and might attract flies.

Some kids aren't supposed to have sugar, and they could not get a drink.

If the soda pop was splashed on people, it might stain their clothes.

Kids might have to pay to get a drink.

Accept other answers that describe the weaknesses of the fountain.

Edward de Bono / Six Thinking Hats for Schools / K-2 Resource Book
Copyright 1991. McQuaig Group / Published by Perfection Learning Corporation

Additional Practice Activities

After introducing the black hat, try the following suggestions for integrating the black hat into other lessons throughout the week. These are only guidelines. Modify or add to them to make the activities relevant and interesting for the children in your classroom.

1. Read aloud a story in which a character makes a plan that goes awry. As you read, ask children to use their black hats to tell what is wrong with the character's plan. For example, you might share the story ''The Garden,'' from *Frog and Toad Together* by Arnold Lobel (Harper and Row, 1972). You could ask children to use their black hats to tell what is wrong with the way Toad tries to make his flowers grow. Some additional suggested titles are listed below.

    - *Alfie Gives a Hand* by Shirley Hughes (William Morrow, 1986).

    - *Animals Should Definitely Not Wear Clothing* by Judi Barrett (Atheneum, 1970).

    - *The Big, Fat, Enormous Lie* by Marjorie Weinman Sharmat (E. P. Dutton, 1978).

    - *Bored—Nothing to Do* by Peter Spier (Doubleday, 1978).

    - *Rosie's Walk* by Pat Hutchins (Macmillan, 1968).

2. Write the following paragraph on the chalkboard or on a large sheet of chart paper. Ask children to use black hat thinking to find the sentence that doesn't fit with the rest of the paragraph and tell why. Create additional

paragraphs or use samples from the children's own writing to provide further practice in checking for fit.

> I have a cat named Willie. He catches mice in our backyard. His fur is soft and white. My grandma lives in a white house. Willie sleeps at the end of my bed and purrs.

3. Throughout the week, pose "what if" questions and ask children to respond with black hat thinking. Use the following sentences as examples, or ask children to think of their own "what if" sentences. (You can also use these questions later and invite yellow hat responses.)

> What if the sun were shining all the time—including at night?
>
> What if you had to put money into your TV set to watch the programs?
>
> What if cars had square wheels?

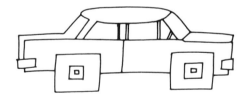

4. Since one function of the black hat is to check for fit, encourage children to use their black hats to check completed assignments. They should look for answers that do not fit (make sense) and check for any other errors.

5. Clip a picture from a current newspaper or news magazine that depicts a social or personal problem, such as homelessness or pollution. Invite children to do some black hat thinking about the picture. Encourage them to observe the bad things about that situation, such as negative consequences for humans or the environment.

6. Display a list of school or classroom rules, or invite children to list the rules that exist. Point out that these rules were created to protect students and teachers from problems and dangers. Select one rule for discussion purposes. Encourage children to use their black thinking hats to think about what could go wrong if this rule was not followed. Work through one or two more examples with the class.

   Invite children to illustrate the other rules to show what might happen if the rules were not obeyed. Provide large sheets of paper, markers, paint, crayons, and other art supplies. Encourage children to include the bad points about the situations they are describing. Some children might be interested in illustrating other kinds of rules as well, such as bicycle safety tips or fire safety rules. Display the finished products in the classroom or hallway.

Summary

Remember . . .

The black hat looks for weak points and problems.

The black hat always provides a reason *why* something will not work.

The black hat asks *What is wrong with this?*

Yellow can mean sunshine and looking on the bright side of things. When children use their yellow thinking hats, they will be thinking about the good points, or benefits, of a plan or an idea.

When we wear the yellow hat, we tell *why* something is good or *why* it will work. There must be a reason behind the statement.

Very often, the yellow hat deals with the future. A suggestion is made or a solution is offered. Because the benefits being claimed are going to come about in the future, we cannot be sure about anything. But we must have good reasons for believing that these benefits will come through.

The yellow hat can also apply to the past. For instance, we might want to find the benefits of something that happened long ago or just last week.

The yellow hat is discussed in more detail in the following teacher notes. Activities for teaching the yellow hat begin on page 38.

THE YELLOW HAT

What are the good points here?

What are the benefits here?

TEACHER NOTES · Yellow Hat

The following description is intended to serve as background for teacher reference. Consult it when needed to clarify how the yellow hat may be used and overused.

Uses of the Yellow Hat

The uses of the yellow hat can be divided into four areas, which overlap quite a bit:

1. Good points

2. Benefits

3. Reasons why an idea will work

4. Likelihood

The following sections discuss these areas in more detail.

Good Points

With the yellow hat, we think of the good points in an idea or situation. The good points of a design could be called the "strong points."

The good points may not be enough to ensure that something will work or prove to be a good choice. Suppose we see a car that is a wonderful green color—we think this color is a good point. But the inside of the car is cramped and the car uses too much fuel. Suddenly, the green color seems irrelevant.

It is important to be able to pick out the good points even when there are very few or there are many more bad or dangerous points. If the good points are of great value, we may decide that it is worth coping with the difficulties or risking the dangers in order to pursue the idea.

Benefits

Yellow hat thinking is a deliberate effort to find benefits—just as a hungry fox makes a great effort to hunt prey or a goat on a rocky mountainside spends all day look-ing for tufts of grass to eat. This effort is important because the benefits may not be obvious. Trying to find them may turn up benefits that no one else has noticed. That sort of thinking has been the basis for many a fortune.

There is also a need to look at how the benefits arise and at the nature of the benefits. Do the benefits arise from some special circumstances over which we have no control (for example, an anonymous benefactor donates money to buy more books for the library)? Also, are the benefits likely to be long lasting? They may depend on some circumstance which will soon change. But even if the benefits are short-lived, we may still value them.

Another essential question is, who gets the benefits from an idea? It is normal for the person who suggested the idea to benefit. A scientist may enjoy the satisfaction of having developed a new theory or may be involved in the profits of patenting an idea for a new invention.

In many cases, it is also usual for the person on the receiving end of the idea to benefit. A politician suggests a new law. This must benefit those who are going to vote for the politician. The politician in turn benefits from increased prestige and also future votes.

In addition to the benefits for the initiator and receiver of the idea, there also may be benefits to third parties. The decision to build a new school in a town will ultimately benefit the children and teachers using the school themselves. But it will also provide more jobs in the construction industry while the school is being built. In addition, having the new school may cause more families to move into the area and improve the real estate market. So it is useful to look not only at the intended benefits but also at those that develop even if unintended.

Types of Benefits

There are many types of benefits, and it is useful to go over them from time to time. In this way, you can be more sensitive to possible benefits.

Simplicity: An idea may make something simpler, such as a simpler hypothesis or a simpler way to solve a math problem. In general, if something can be made simpler, it will benefit us by requiring less effort, being more effective, and reducing errors.

Effectiveness: Some ideas have the benefit of allowing us to achieve what we set out to do in a stronger way. The effect we get is stronger.

Efficiency: An idea that improves output without increasing input or gives the same output with less input offers a benefit.

Acceptability: It is a benefit if an idea is one that people are more likely to accept than other ideas. More people will accept the idea with less persuasion.

Opportunity: If an idea will put us in a position where there are now more opportunities, then that is a benefit.

Lower cost: It is a benefit if an idea results in less cost in terms of money, time, effort, or hassle.

Lower risk: It is a benefit if a new idea reduces dangers and uncertainties.

Increased values: If an idea brings an increase in existing values (more security, peace, better health) or offers something new that we value (new friends, new interests), then this is a benefit.

So there are many types of benefits to search for with the yellow hat.

TEACHER NOTES · Yellow Hat

Why an Idea Will Work

This is the answer to the black hat criticism: Will it work? The yellow hat must always set out the full logical reasons why something is expected to work.

"This will work because . . . "

These reasons may be based on any of the following:

information ("Statistics show that the average age is . . . ")

principles of physics, chemistry, nature, etc. ("If we curve it there, it will be stronger.")

experience ("Whenever prices are about to go up, people always hurry out to buy more.")

plain logic ("If this investment is shared, each person pays less.")

The yellow hat thinker must be able to meet the objections of the black hat thinker. There may still remain a difference based on experience or different information, but there must be an answer to all objections.

As we shall see later, there is a big difference between green hat thinking and yellow hat thinking. Green hat thinking puts forward suggestions and possibilities. There is only a vague hint that they may work (and sometimes not even that). The purpose of the green hat is to come up with ideas or to get some proposals on the table. The yellow hat then takes each of these proposals and tries to show how it could be made to work. This aspect of yellow hat thinking is more constructive than judgmental.

Likelihood

It is difficult to be certain about the future. It is difficult to prove that a venture will work or that a proposed solution really will solve a problem. Nevertheless, entrepreneurs do have to take initiative, and people do have to make decisions about problems. We cannot wait for certainty when there can be no certainty about the future.

Sometimes we can be reasonably sure about an idea, and when we are, then we can discuss our idea under the category of why an idea will work. At other times, we are not so sure. We can then think in terms of the degree of likelihood that something will work. Yellow hat thinking is only concerned with a high degree of likelihood (perhaps 70 percent or over). Lesser degrees of likelihood would come under the green hat, which deals in possibilities.

The yellow hat also seeks to establish the basis for likelihood with questions such as these: What is the evidence? What are the clues? What are the trends? What are the competing possibilities?

With likelihood, we are dealing in risks because something may not turn out as we had claimed or wished. There may even be danger, harm, loss, or damage involved. If this *harm* risk is low or absent, however, we might choose to go ahead with a project even if the *success* likelihood is lower than usual. If the *harm* risk is high, then we should want a much higher likelihood of success.

Purposes for Using the Yellow Hat

The three main purposes for using the yellow hat are

1. Assessing value

2. Extracting benefits

3. Making something work

First, we can use the yellow hat as part of an assessment and then move on to the black hat. The yellow hat part of the assessment involves listing the good points and the benefits in the proposal or idea. The black hat then examines the weak points, difficulties, and dangers. Using the yellow hat in this way is part of making a judgment.

Second, the yellow hat can be used in a deliberate effort to extract some benefit or good points from something which has generally been thought unworkable, unattractive, or even a disaster. This yellow hat activity is not going to result in an assessment. What is extracted may, however, be of value. It is a sort of "mining" use of the yellow hat.

Third, the yellow hat can be used in an effort to make something work. This is the constructive use of the yellow hat. For example, after the green hat has put forward possibilities, the yellow hat may seek to give these a solid basis. This is an active process, not just an assessment. The constructive use of the yellow hat also seeks to establish likelihood.

Overuse

It is possible to be overly optimistic and "Pollyanna" in attitude. It is possible to believe that something will work only because you wish it to work. Or it is possible to be too optimistic as to likelihood.

Another type of overuse is to focus entirely on the yellow hat and to ignore the valuable contribution of the black hat.

Summary of the Yellow Hat

The key words to describe the uses of the yellow hat are *good points, benefits, workability,* and *likelihood.* The three main purposes for using the yellow hat are to make assessments, extract benefits, and think of ways to make something work. The overall questions to ask are *What are the good points?* or *What are the benefits?*

The Yellow Hat

Follow these steps to introduce the yellow hat: lead-in, explanation, and practice.

Lead-in

Help children recall whatever they can remember about the black hat. Explain that they will now have a chance to explore a second hat. Do not identify the color of this hat until after the lead-in.

Then ask children some of the following questions:

What are the good points of being an only child? (You probably have your own room; you get all the attention; you don't have to share things.)

What are the good points of having lots of brothers and sisters? (You have each other to play with; you can help each other when there are difficulties; you can borrow things from each other.)

If bicycles were the only vehicles allowed on the streets, what would the benefits be? (It would be safer to ride; kids could go more places; it would save on gas; the air would be cleaner; the streets wouldn't be so crowded; bike stores would make more money.)

In all cases, ask repeatedly, "What are the good points?" or "What are the benefits?"

Older children may be able to create their own examples of things that have good points or benefits. Invite them to do so, then have them trade items and discover the good points.

Explanation

After the lead-in, ask children which hat they have been using. If necessary, review all of the hats so that they can remember the choices. Point out that yellow hat thinking finds reasons why something is good. As you model the use of the yellow hat, identify specific benefits in the topics you're discussing.

"My yellow hat idea is that if we take recess early today, we may get outside before it rains."

"Here's my yellow hat thinking on having two at a time in the learning center—if there are only two, it won't be overcrowded, and yet you'll have a partner to work with."

Practice

After the lead-in or on another day, have children work individually, in small groups, or as a class to complete the following **Put On Your Yellow Thinking Hat** reproducible. Read the description and directions aloud. Then invite children to put on their yellow hats to think about what might be good about having two faces.

As children share their responses, write their comments on a large sheet of chart paper using a yellow marker or on a sheet of yellow paper using a dark marker. Post the completed chart in the room along with the black hat response chart. This will help children remember which type of thinking is represented by each hat.

Consider having children wear yellow paper hats or visors as you discuss this new thinking hat. Hat patterns are provided on pages 102 and 103.

Put On Your Yellow Thinking Hat

Directions

Imagine that you have another face on the back of your head. Put on your yellow hat and think about all of the things that would be good about having two faces.

List your ideas in the space below or share your ideas with the class.

Remember, when you wear your yellow hat, you are looking for the **good** points or how something could help you.

Edward de Bono / Six Thinking Hats for Schools / K-2 Resource Book
Copyright 1991. McQuaig Group / Published by Perfection Learning Corporation

Put On Your Yellow Thinking Hat · Teacher Page

Put On Your Yellow Thinking Hat

Directions

Imagine that you have another face on the back of your head. Put on your yellow hat and think about all of the things that would be good about having two faces.

List your ideas in the space below or share your ideas with the class.

Remember, when you wear your yellow hat, you are looking for the **good** points or how something could help you.

Sample yellow hat comments:

You could see where you have been as well as where you are going.

No one could sneak up behind you and scare you.

You could talk and eat at the same time.

You could swim with one face in the water and the other face out of the water doing the breathing.

You could whistle and sing along at the same time.

Accept other answers that describe the benefits of having two faces.

40

Additional Practice Activities

After introducing the yellow hat, try the following suggestions for integrating the yellow hat into other lessons throughout the week. These are only guidelines. Modify or add to them to make the activities relevant and interesting for the children in your classroom.

1. Pose a question about a topic you are studying in science or social studies. Ask children to use yellow hat thinking to consider the good points of the situation being discussed. Sample questions are listed below.

   What are the good points about eating healthy foods?

   What would be some of the good points about living in the city? in the country?

   What would have been some good points about being alive when the dinosaurs were living?

   What are the good points of having your skeleton on the outside of your body, like insects do?

2. At the beginning of each day, post one of the following questions on the chalkboard or overhead. Give children several minutes to consider their responses. Or hold a class discussion at the end of the day.

   What are the good points of being tall?

   What are the good points of being short?

   If dogs could be taught to speak, what would the benefits be?

   What are the good points of learning to write many different words?

   Turtles can live to be 100 years old. What would be some of the good points of living that long?

3. Offer each child a copy of the soda pop fountain reproducible found on page 30. This time, ask children to use their yellow hats to think about the good points of this invention. Or display the black hat "what if" questions (see page 33, **Additional Practice Activities**) and ask children to consider the good points of each situation described.

4. Share a story in which a character is doing yellow hat thinking. As you read, encourage children to discuss the examples of yellow hat thinking in the story. Some suggested titles are listed below.

   - *Gilberto and the Wind* by Marie Hall Ets (Viking Press, 1963).

   - *Here I Am, an Only Child* by Marlene Fanta Shyer (Scribner, 1985).

   - *If the Dinosaurs Came Back* by Bernard Most (Harcourt Brace Jovanovich, 1978).

   - *My Mom Travels a Lot* by Caroline Feller Bauer (Warne, 1981).

   - *Snow Is Falling* by Franklyn M. Branley (Crowell, 1963).

   - *Stevie* by John Steptoe (Harper and Row, 1969).

5. Play a sentence completion game. Arrange children into pairs. Have one partner say or write part of a yellow hat sentence: "Carrots are good for you because . . ." Let the other child finish the sentence by giving a reason why that is true: " . . . they have vitamins that your body needs to be healthy."

6. Point out that many advertisements and commercials are written by people who use yellow hat thinking. The ad writers try to mention all of the good points about a product so that customers will want to buy it. Invite children to create advertisements for their favorite toys, books, foods, or games. Provide large sheets of paper, markers, paints, crayons, and other art supplies. Encourage children to include the good points about the items they are advertising. Display the finished products in the classroom or hallway.

7. Change is often difficult for young children. Use a recent school event or circumstance to illustrate that although change may sometimes be upsetting, there are many good things that can be brought about by change. Invite children to do yellow hat thinking about the change. For example, getting a new student teacher may mean more help in the classroom and another person to share ideas with. Good things about a change in the daily schedule may be more time for reading in the morning or not having to go to gym class right after lunch.

Summary

Remember . . .

Yellow hat thinking looks for ways an idea might work or succeed.

The yellow hat always provides a reason *why* something will work.

The yellow hat asks *What are the good points?* or *What are the benefits?*

THE WHITE HAT

What information do we have?

What information do we need?

How do we get the information we need?

Τhe white hat is for finding the facts. When you explain the white hat to children, ask them to think about the white pages of a dictionary, a computer printout, or a newspaper. Remind children of the difference between a fact and an opinion and point out that white hat thinking deals only with facts. There are no suggestions, ideas, or arguments. Feelings, hunches, and intuitions do not come into it. Just information.

In ordinary thinking, we are using information all the time, and we do not need to put on a white hat every time we bring some piece of information into our thinking. The purpose of the white hat is to provide a means for directly focusing on information from time to time.

> "No more arguments. Put on your white hats and think about the facts. Tell me just the facts about what happened."

The white hat also allows us to be clear about the information that we need but do not yet have.

> "As we found out yesterday, Brownie, our hamster, is going to have babies. Let's put on our white hats and think of all the facts we need to know to get ready for her new family."

White hat thinking is not just a matter of taking facts out of a book and putting them onto paper. The white hat also evaluates the usefulness of information. Is the source reliable? Are these facts relevant? What else do we need to know? Thinking is involved.

The white hat is discussed in more detail in the following teacher notes. Activities for teaching the white hat begin on page 50.

TEACHER NOTES · White Hat

The following description is intended to serve as background for teacher reference. Consult it when needed to clarify how the white hat may be used and overused.

Uses of the White Hat

The main uses of the white hat can be summarized as three questions:

1. What information do we have?

2. What information do we need?

3. How do we get the information we need?

We can visualize ourselves as explorers wearing the white hat to make a map. We fill in the areas which are known and identify the areas where more information is needed.

Information We Have

A good place to begin when using the white hat is to make note of all the information, formal and informal, that is readily available. What information do we have? The answer will give us an inventory.

Formal kinds of information can include reports, statistics, and facts. There are also "informal" kinds of information which arise from personal experience.

"Bill told me that he does not like to travel."

Describing our own feelings on a subject is red hat thinking. But reporting how others have said that they feel is white hat thinking. In such a case, we are reporting what we know—in this case, we know what Bill said—and not putting forth our own feelings.

While looking at the information that we have, we could ask other questions:

What is relevant?

What is most important?

How valid is this?

Assessing the relevance and importance of information is not easy to do at the beginning. If certain courses of action or possibilities arise, we may want to go back and look at the information again. New events and new knowledge can change the relevance and importance of information. So an early assessment of these matters is only tentative. The information must be kept available in case this assessment has to change. Otherwise, we shall simply be reinforcing the ideas with which we started out.

As we are gathering information, we may find reason to challenge its validity. If information is not true or correct, it simply should not be used. So along the way, we should be asking if our information is true or correct.

Challenging the validity of the information is important. However, a full challenge to the validity of information is a matter for black hat thinking: checking evidence, checking logic, and so forth. This black hat challenge is not carried out during the white hat thinking. Instead, there are three things that can be done:

1. Note the challenge and return to it later with specific black hat thinking.

2. Note the disagreement or doubt so that this becomes part of the information.

3. Jot down the original and the differing information so that both versions are available. If the issue becomes important later, both can be checked out.

For example, someone claims that the number of murders per year in the United States is 28,000 and someone else claims it is 15,000. We record both versions and then get on with white hat thinking.

In this way, the flow of white hat thinking continues. If there is a constant switching between white and black hats, the process becomes very messy. So proceed to make the map, but put question marks where needed.

In Japanese prints and Chinese paintings, the space is as important as the figures. In white hat thinking, we need to focus on the information that is not there. We need to be aware of and define the gaps in the information. What is missing?

Information We Need

In Japanese prints and Chinese paintings, the space is as important as the figures. In white hat thinking, we need to focus on the information that is not there. We need to be aware of and define the gaps in the information. What is missing?

A *gap* is not the same as a *need*. For instance, in a series of annual files, some years may be missing. This would be a gap in information. It may turn out that missing information is not needed. However, we should be in the habit of noting gaps in information. With *needs*, we are conscious that

TEACHER NOTES · White Hat

we do need the information and it is not there:

"We don't have enough information to make a decision. We need to know how much plan B would cost."

As, with the relevance and importance of information, needs are not easy to assess at the beginning. In fact, we can probably assess them only in a general way.

"Before starting to think about this matter, we need to know the following things."

This statement is a general assessment of information needed.

In classic detective stories, white hat thinking is always featured. The great detective typically defines a crucial piece of information that will solve the case. In the same way, as our thinking about a situation unfolds, we constantly check new ideas against available information. By checking, we may find an information need that was not apparent at the beginning. It suddenly becomes vital to know something.

Needs should always be defined as specifically as possible, even if the need is general. There are two sorts of need:

1. We need more information in general about a particular area. "We need more information about dolphins."

2. We need to check something specific. "How many species of dolphins are there?" "Is it true that dolphins never sleep?" We need an answer or want to check whether something is true.

Getting the Information We Need

Having defined the information we need, we then set out to get it.

Basically, there are three ways of doing this:

1. By asking questions
2. By interpreting and making inferences
3. By consulting sources

Asking questions. Questions have a powerful way of focusing attention and getting information. Choosing and phrasing questions are key skills of any courtroom lawyer. These skills are also needed in using the white hat.

Two basic types of questions that will help us use the white hat are *fishing* questions and *shooting* questions. (See my *CoRT Thinking Program,* section V, published by SRA, for more information.)

Fishing questions are used when we need more information. We "fish" when we put down the bait but do not know what we shall catch:

"Can you describe the scene of the accident?"

"What else do you know about Ms. Hudson?"

Fishing questions are used when we need more information. We "fish" when we put down the bait but do not know what we shall catch.

Shooting questions are aimed at a specific target. After you fire, you know at once whether or not you have hit the target. So the shooting question is quite specific:

"How old are you?"

Shooting questions are aimed at a specific target. After you fire, you know at once whether or not you have hit the target.

"How much does this cost?"

Note too that shooting questions very often require a simple yes or no answer:

"Were you at home on Monday evening?"

"Did she sign the agreement?"

Interpreting and making inferences. With interpretation and inference, we try to extract something more from the information in front of us. This is similar to what detectives and scientists do through deduction: "If this is so, then this must also be so . . ." By a logical process, we move from the evidence or clues to some new information that is hidden within the available information.

Inference is meant to be based on logical deduction, but interpretation may be a matter of opinion. At some point, interpretation can move into green hat thinking in which we offer a possible hypothesis or explanation.

Interpretation also covers "reading between the lines" and noting points of significance. In the famous Sherlock Holmes case, *The Hound of the Baskervilles,* the fact that the dog did not bark was a key point. Likewise, if there are four people at a meeting and one of them says nothing, this too may be important. Or if certain uses of a new plastic are mentioned but a

TEACHER NOTES · White Hat

possible common use is not, this may be a significant omission.

By working to interpret and make inferences, we are able to get more information from what is available. There is a skill to doing this, and with practice, we can become adept at it.

Consulting sources. There was a time when an educated person could know almost all the knowledge there was to know. Today there is so much information and it is growing so rapidly that there is no way anyone can know it all. We always need to know a certain amount of background information, but beyond that, the most important thing to know is where to go to get information.

Already, many educators realize that teaching students how to get information has become a key function of education. This is happening not only at the university level but at the elementary and secondary levels as well. The framework of the white hat can be used to reinforce this point: If the information is not in front of us, and if we can't extract the information by questions, inference, and interpretation, then we have to go to some source. Here are a few basic sources.

Experts: These are people who know a lot about a subject. An expert may give the required answer or direct us to another expert or some other source.

Printed matter and audiovisual materials: There are standard references and journals in just about every field. Likewise, there are some excellent films, videos, or audiocassettes that contain a wealth of information. Many of these sources can be discovered through libraries. Knowing how to use a library, then, can open many doors.

Computer data banks: Today much information has been put on computers and can be obtained by entering the right network and asking questions. In the future, this access to information will become more valuable and convenient.

Today there is so much information and it is growing so rapidly that there is no way anyone can know it all. The most important thing to know is where to go to get information.

Purposes for Using the White Hat

The two main purposes for using the white hat are to

1. Stimulate thinking

2. Check thinking

At the beginning of many thinking tasks, we need information to get started. This information, in turn, will help us develop ideas (green hat thinking). At any subsequent point in our thinking, we can go back to the information to stimulate further ideas. This is like the scientist who uses the results from an experiment to form a hypothesis. We need information to start thinking. Without information, there could be no thinking.

Once we have the ideas, however, we need to see whether or not they are workable in the situation. So we go back to look at the available information. For example, a business

would do market research to see if there is a market for a new product. An archaeologist who has formed a theory about civilization X will look around to see if the available information and/or evidence supports that theory. The difference between a wild idea and a practical one is that the practical idea fits the available information; the wild one does not.

Overuse

It may seem impossible that there could be overuse of the white hat. How could we have too much information?

However, there are times when some people will refuse to do any thinking. They will just ask for more information in the hope that this information will do the thinking for them. This, of course, is not always practical. For instance, a doctor may need to act as a matter of urgency, such as in the case of suspected meningitis. It is impractical to wait for the test results because then it may be too late to save the patient. In another example, a businessperson may want to move quickly on an idea. If he or she waits until all the information is obvious, then it will also be obvious to the competitors. There are times, then, when the white hat should be put aside.

Summary of the White Hat

Some key words to keep in mind when teaching the white hat are *information, gaps, needs, questions, interpretation,* and *sources.* The two main purposes for using the white hat are to stimulate thinking and to check thinking. The basic questions to keep in mind when using the white hat are these three: *What information do we have? What information do we need? How do we get the information we need?*

STUDENT ACTIVITIES

The White Hat

 Follow these steps to introduce the white hat: lead-in, explanation, and practice.

Lead-in

Help children recall whatever they can remember about the black and yellow hats. Explain that they will now be taking a closer look at a third hat. Do not identify the color of this hat until after the lead-in.

Display a photograph or picture and ask children to tell you some facts about it. Explain that they are not to tell how they *feel* about the picture or things that *might* be true, only the observable facts.

Then ask children some of the following questions:

What are some facts about this classroom? (There is a door at the front; there are 32 small desks; there is 1 teacher's desk; there are 3 bulletin boards; the windows have blinds.)

What are some facts about the playground? (It is covered with gravel; it has a slide and swings and monkey bars; you can play tetherball there; you can shoot baskets.)

What are some facts about our city?

What are some facts about our country?

In all cases, distinguish between facts and other kinds of points like feelings, opinions, and suggestions.

Explanation

After the lead-in, ask children which hat they have been using. As before, review all six hats if needed so that they can remember the choices. When the white hat has been established, point out that white hat thinking looks for facts and information. As you model the use of the white hat, point out the information you are reporting or seeking.

"Putting on my white hat, I think that we need some *information.* We need to know what time the assembly begins. Let's call the office and find out."

"I have some white hat facts to share with you. Tomorrow is open house. You are welcome to come to school with your parents. Only the south doors will be open. The south doors are the front doors by the gymnasium."

Practice

After the lead-in or on another day, have children work individually, in small groups, or as a class to complete the following **Put On Your White Thinking Hat** reproducible. Read the description and directions aloud. Then invite children to put on their white hats to think about the facts they would like to have if they were to get a new pet. Invite children to wear white hats or paper visors while they complete this activity.

As children share their responses, write their comments on a large sheet of white chart paper using a dark marker. Display this response record along with those for the black and yellow hats.

Consider having children wear white paper hats or visors as you discuss this thinking hat. Hat patterns are provided on pages 102 and 103.

Put On Your White Thinking Hat

Edward de Bono / Six Thinking Hats for Schools / K-2 Resource Book
Copyright 1991. McQuaig Group / Published by Perfection Learning Corporation

Put On Your White Thinking Hat - Teacher Page

Put On Your White Thinking Hat

Directions

Pretend that you have just learned that someone has bought you a new pet. It is inside this box. Put on your white hat and think of all the facts you would like to know about this pet.

Write your questions in the space below or share your responses with the class.

Sample white hat comments:

What kind of pet is it?

Where did it come from?

What does it eat?

How big is it?

Does it bite?

Where will I keep it?

What color is it?

Accept other questions that ask for information about the new pet. Distinguish between questions for information and questions that would elicit opinion.

Edward de Bono / Six Thinking Hats for Schools / K-2 Resource Book
Copyright 1991. McQuaig Group / Published by Perfection Learning Corporation

Additional Practice Activities

After introducing the white hat, try the following suggestions for integrating the white hat into other lessons throughout the week. These are only guidelines. Modify or add to them to make the activities relevant and interesting for the children in your classroom.

1. Play I Spy or Twenty Questions. Tell children that you are thinking of an object and ask them to guess what it might be. Invite them to ask questions to find out facts about the object. (''Is it round?'' ''Does it hang on the wall?'' ''Is it something a person can wear?'') Explain that you will only respond to fact questions that can be answered with ''yes'' or ''no.'' When a child correctly guesses the object, he or she may take a turn at selecting an object and answering questions about it.

2. Ask children to write down five facts about the classroom—but not about the people in the room. Encourage them to look around as much as they like. Then ask volunteers to read their facts aloud.

   Help children distinguish between facts and other kinds of points like feelings, opinions, and suggestions. For instance, ''The library corner is fun'' (red hat) could be reworded to make it factual: ''The library corner has big beanbag chairs and lots of shelves with books.'' ''The playground does not have enough swings on it'' (black hat) could be rephrased: ''There are four swings on the playground.''

3. Invite volunteers to tell all the facts they know about the topic currently being discussed in a content-area lesson, such as science or social studies. Write each fact on the chalkboard or overhead as it is offered. This is an excellent way to review material that has already been covered before introducing new concepts.

   You may also want to include this information on a chart that has been divided into three columns: Things We Know, Things We Want to Know, and Things We

Have Learned. Children are asked to rely on prior knowledge to complete the first column. After they have generated questions for the second column, ask children to use white hat thinking to decide where to look for information that will help them answer those questions. Then help children do research and list the new facts they have discovered in the third column.

4. Ask each child to write a topic on a sheet of paper. Then have children trade papers and list at least five facts about the topic they receive.

5. Share a nonfiction book with children relevant to their interest level. Ask children to work individually, in small groups, or as a class to list facts they learned from the book.

6. Have each child fill in a blank calendar for the current month, or display a large printed calendar on the overhead or bulletin board. Ask white hat questions about the month. These could be designed for oral or written response. Sample questions are listed below.

   What is today's date?

   How many days are in a week?

   What day will come after today?

   What day came before today?

   What holidays are in this month?

   How many days of school will we have this month?

7. Offer each child a large sheet of drawing paper. On one half of the page, encourage children to draw their self-portraits. On the other half, invite them to list five white hat facts about themselves. Collect the papers and

keep them, or display them on a classroom bulletin board. When the red hat is being introduced, children can add red hat comments. ("I like swimming." "I don't like pizza.") The individual papers can then be compiled into a class book or used for a "Getting to Know You" display.

8. Play a trivia game. Challenge each child to come up with five white hat questions about the school, the community, or a subject area. Collect the questions. Then divide the class into teams, or exchange questions with another class and see which group can answer the most questions.

9. Have children work together to produce a class newspaper. Each day, assign a few children to write about the day's activities. Help them edit their reports to make sure that only facts are included. Arrange children into groups to insure that each child will be able to contribute to the paper. At the end of the week, compile all of the columns into a newspaper and provide each child with a copy.

Summary

Remember . . .

The white hat is for finding information.

White hat thinking deals only with facts.

The white hat asks *What information do we have?*
What information do we need? and
How do we get the information that we need?

THE GREEN HAT

*What ideas
do we have?*

The green hat is for creative thinking. When you explain the green hat to children, ask them to think about green grass and forests and gardens. Green stands for things that grow and take on new shapes and forms. Think of a plant with shoots and branches. Think of alternatives.

Black hat and yellow hat thinking are not enough because they are for "reactive" thinking. We use these hats to react to something that is put before us. We judge or assess it. But we need another kind of thinking to generate ideas. We can't judge or assess an idea until someone has generated it.

The green hat indicates a creative attitude. This means moving forward to possibilities and new ideas. The white hat deals with *what is now*. The green hat deals with *what may be next*, the possibilities.

At the moment we put forward an idea, it is only a possibility. Then we proceed to develop the idea and to check it out against the information and against our objectives. We bring in the yellow hat and black hat thinking to strengthen the idea. Finally we assess the idea and compare it to alternative ideas.

The generative green hat stage is the possibility stage. This is the stage of suggestions and proposals.

The green hat is discussed in more detail in the following teacher notes. Activities for teaching the green hat begin on page 61.

TEACHER NOTES · Green Hat

The following description is intended to serve as background for teacher reference. Consult it when needed to clarify how the green hat may be used and overused.

Green Hat Situations

There are many types of thinking situations which call for the green hat.

Action. We are faced with a problem or we have set ourselves a task. What do we do? With green hat thinking, we can generate alternative solutions or alternative courses of action. We might do this by analyzing the problem or looking at similar problems. Or we might try using creative thinking.

Explanation. Something has happened. People have behaved in a certain way, there are scientific observations—what is the explanation? With green hat thinking, we put forward a possible explanation or hypothesis. Then we seek to check this out.

The purpose of the explanation is ultimately to allow us to move forward. We seek to explain an illness in order to see how we might treat, cure, and prevent that illness. If we can explain what motivates students to learn, then we might know how to design better strategies for teaching them.

Forecasting. It is difficult to be certain about the future. So we have to imagine possibilities. We can use green hat thinking to create alternative scenarios or future states of the world, community, family, or our own lives.

Whenever we make a decision, there are consequences. We need to be able to look at these possible consequences before we act. At this specific point, the black hat does some green hat thinking. It imagines possible future dangers and difficulties.

Design. In design and invention, we produce something new to fit a need. Using the green hat, we generate possible designs and then examine them in terms of aesthetics, cost, function, and ease of manufacture. Designers rarely come up with only one design. Many design possibilities are usually considered.

Hypothesis, Speculation, Provocation, and Lateral Thinking—Fundamentals of the Green Hat

When wearing the green hat, we use words like *suppose, maybe, perhaps, what if,* and *possibly.* All these indicate a possibility and a lack of certainty. We leap ahead of the information and lay out a possible idea. Using the new idea, the mind can view the situation in a new way.

The need to find ways to leap ahead is very important. The mind can only see what it is prepared to see. This is because of the way the mind works as a self-organizing information system. (For more detail on this point, see my book *I Am Right—You Are Wrong.*) Three ways to move ahead of the existing information are by forming hypotheses, speculating, and making provocative statements.

A hypothesis is supposed to be the most reasonable explanation. A scientist uses green hat thinking to generate a hypothesis. This hypothesis is then checked out by designing experiments to show that the hypothesis is wrong. The more a scientist and colleagues fail to disprove a hypothesis, the stronger it becomes.

A speculation is less reasonable than a hypothesis. It involves more guesswork.

"What if we look at it this way . . . "

"What if this was not caused by heat but by the increased noise . . . "

"Suppose the murderer did not flee as everyone believes. Suppose he or she is still around?"

A provocation goes even beyond speculation. Provocations help us dislodge our minds from their usual patterns. (See my book *Lateral Thinking* published by Harper & Row.) We use the special word *PO* (provocative operation) to signal a provocation.

"PO: Cars should have square wheels."

With provocation there is no pretense at reasonableness. A PO statement may appear to be complete nonsense.

Lateral thinking is a term I invented in 1967 to describe the thinking that is used to cut across the patterns of perception formed by the self-organizing behavior of the brain. The technical background for this is described in *I Am Right—You Are Wrong.* There are a number of specific lateral thinking techniques which can be used deliberately in order to generate new ideas.

One very simple technique is the use of a random word. We simply take any word (preferably a noun) and put it alongside the subject for which a new idea is needed. For example we might say "study PO frog" to get some new ideas about how to teach students better study habits. From this juxtaposition, we get the idea of having students use headings in a chapter to hop through the text, previewing the material they are going to read.

Random words are extremely easy to use. The process works because a random word allows us to enter our patterns of thinking at

TEACHER NOTES · Green Hat

a new point and so increases the chances of opening up new patterns. (For more information about the educational uses of lateral thinking, see part IV of my *CoRT Thinking Program* published by SRA.)

If the techniques of lateral thinking are known or available, they can be used as part of green hat thinking. However, the techniques are not essential since green hat thinking covers all attempts to be creative.

Purpose for Using the Green Hat

Green hat thinking is not only concerned with *new* ideas. Green hat thinking is concerned with the generation of *any* ideas. If someone comes up with a very old idea to solve a problem, this can still be green hat thinking. The main purpose of green hat thinking is to be generative, productive, and to move thinking forward. Finding completely new ideas is only one means of making progress.

Uses of the Green Hat

We can look at four main activities of green hat thinking:

1. Generating reactive ideas
2. Generating starting ideas
3. Generating further and better ideas
4. Generating new ideas

Generating Reactive Ideas

When an idea is presented, we can use the green hat in a reactive way. We can ask, "What is interesting about this idea?" The word *interesting* indicates a creative exploration to see what the idea suggests or what the idea leads to. We use the given idea as a starting point in order to explore creatively.

We can use the green hat reactively to modify or improve an idea that has been presented. We can do this even before the black hat has pointed out weaknesses in the idea.

> "That is a good idea, but it would be even better if we let people choose their own reward."

Generating Starting Ideas

On our own or as part of a group, we set out to think about something. We use the white hat first to collect the information. Then what? We need some starting ideas. The green hat is used to lay out some starting ideas. Sometimes the starting ideas are easy, obvious, and conventional. Sometimes it is difficult to get any ideas at all.

These starting ideas do not have to be proven or sure things before they can be put forward. They are only possibilities. Such ideas are then checked against the information and developed with yellow hat and black hat thinking.

Generating Further or Better Ideas

There are times when we do have some ideas, but they do not seem very satisfactory. We may not be able to choose between the obvious alternatives because none of them seems of great value. So instead of pushing ahead with the existing ideas, we make an effort to see if there are further ideas and further alternatives. We may never find them, but we make the effort.

> "We seem to be bogged down here. Let's put on our green hats and try to find some new approaches."

Even when there is no obvious need to look for further alternatives, it is a good thinking habit to make some effort to see if there might be other ideas. Quite often an idea seems satisfactory but with a little effort a much better idea can be found. There is no reason at all to suppose that the first satisfactory idea you find is the best solution to the problem.

Generating New Ideas

There are times when we really do want new ideas. This may be for reasons of competitive advantage: we need new products; we want to set up a new business. It may be because the old ways simply do not work any longer. In either case, we specifically set ourselves the task of generating *new* ideas. This is where the deliberate techniques of lateral thinking could be used (such as the random word technique).

Overuse

Creativity and the green hat can be overused. To ignore sound conventional ideas and to search only for new and exotic ideas may be an overuse of the green hat. To want to work only in the area of possibilities and to refuse to come down to practical realities is also overuse. To continue to look for further ideas when immediate action needs to be taken is overuse. To wait for a magic new idea to solve all problems is also overuse.

The green hat, like all the other hats, has its role, its place and its use. In general we do not use the green hat nearly enough, whereas we tend to overuse the black hat.

Summary of the Green Hat

Some key words related to the green hat are *creative, generative, possibilities,* and *alternatives.* Green hat thinking can help when we need to take an action, provide an explanation, forecast an outcome, or design something new to fit a need. Forming hypotheses, speculating, and thinking laterally are three green hat thinking tools. We use the green hat to generate reactive ideas, starting ideas, further ideas, and new ideas. The overall question for green hat thinking is *What ideas do we have?*

ollow these steps to introduce the green hat: lead-in, explanation, and practice.

Lead-in

Invite children to put on their white thinking hats and tell you some facts about each hat they have already learned: black, yellow, and white. Explain that today they will begin to explore a fourth hat. As before, do not reveal the color of the hat until after the lead-in.

Make a simple outline drawing on the chalkboard or overhead projector. This might be a circle with a smaller circle inside of it. Ask the class for suggestions as to what the drawing might represent. (It could be a tire, a doughnut, a fat letter *O*, etc.)

Then make another simple drawing and ask what this could be. As children make suggestions, point out that they are thinking of *new ideas, possibilities,* or *alternatives*.

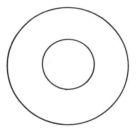 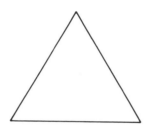

After discussing the drawings, ask students to draw a picture showing how the human head could be improved.

"How would you improve the human head? What ideas do you have?"

Usually this produces eyes on the back of the head, octopus-like tentacles, rearrangement of the hair, bigger ears, etc. Accept all ideas without comment, since the green hat does not evaluate. Invite students to trade pictures, or you might want to display their ideas so that all can see the many *possibilities*.

By Melissa

Explanation

After the lead-in, ask children which hat they have been using. When they have identified the green hat, display a green plant. Ask children to notice the shoots and branches of the plant. Point out that, like the plant, green hat thinking has shoots and branches. Green hat thinkers begin with a topic, and their creative thinking branches off from there in many different directions.

As you model the use of the green hat, point out the fact that you are offering new ideas or possibilities.

"Putting on my green hat, I have a new idea. Why don't we move the salamander's cage over on the bookshelf by the sink? Then we could get water for it without running back and forth across the room."

"Could anyone give me a green hat idea about the tools a fire fighter might need to put out a fire? What are some possibilities?"

Practice

After the lead-in or on another day, have children work in-dividually, in small groups, or as a class to complete the following **Put On Your Green Thinking Hat** reproducible. Read the description and directions aloud. Then invite children to put on their green hats to think about new ideas for the artist's painting.

As children share their responses, record them on a large sheet of chart paper using a green marker or on a large sheet of green paper using a dark marker. Display this chart along with those created for the black, yellow, and white hats.

Consider having children wear green paper hats or visors as you discuss this thinking hat. Hat patterns are provided on pages 102 and 103.

Put On Your Green Thinking Hat

Directions

An artist has just spilled paint in the middle of her canvas. She is going to throw the canvas away but then decides that she could make an interesting painting out of her mistake.

Look at the drop of paint below. Turn the paper any way you want.

Use your green hat and think about the many possible things this shape could become.

Use crayons, markers, or paints to show your new idea.

Edward de Bono / Six Thinking Hats for Schools / K-2 Resource Book
Copyright 1991. McQuaig Group / Published by Perfection Learning Corporation

Put On Your Green Thinking Hat - Teacher Page

You may wish to give each child several copies of the handout so that they are encouraged to come up with several alternatives or possibilities for the painting.

After the drawings are completed, invite volunteers to show and explain their ideas. Then display the drawings on a bulletin board or wall. Observe with the children the many possibilities they created with their green thinking hats.

(Accept all designs. Drawings will vary.)

Additional Practice Activities

After introducing the green hat, try the following suggestions for integrating the green hat into other lessons throughout the week. These are only guidelines. Modify or add to them to make the activities relevant and interesting for the children in your classroom.

1. Share a book in which a character is doing green hat thinking. Discuss the examples of green hat thinking with children as you read. Some suggested titles are listed below.

   - *Miss Nelson Is Missing* by Harry Allard (Houghton Mifflin, 1977).

   - *Old Bear* by Jane Hissy (Philomel, 1986).

   - *A Rainbow of My Own* by Don Freeman (Viking, 1966).

   - *What Happened to Patrick's Dinosaurs?* by Carol Carrick (Clarion, 1986).

   - *Who's in Rabbit's House?* by Verna Aardema (Dial, 1977).

2. Share the book *If I Ran the Zoo* by Dr. Seuss (Random House, 1950). Then ask children to put on their green thinking hats and design a new, improved zoo. Provide pencils, paints, markers, crayons, paper, and other art supplies.

3. Invite children to use green hat thinking to help you solve a classroom problem. For example, if children often forget to put their names on completed assignments, describe the problem to children and ask them to suggest solutions. Encourage children to come up with as many possibilities as they can, whether the ideas are realistic or not. The point of the activity is to generate lots of new ideas.

4. Locate a green file box or cover one with green paper. Then prepare a set of index cards by writing a word or displaying a picture on each card. Invite children to randomly select a given number of cards from the box. Then encourage children to use their green hats to write stories that contain all of the words and pictures they selected.

5. Talk to children about inventors and their inventions. Point out that inventors do a lot of green hat thinking. Offer children the chance to become inventors by providing them with a variety of materials and asking them to invent a gadget that will solve a problem or improve life in some way. Specific suggestions could include inventing a new toy, a new musical instrument, a new cleaning device, or a new tool for the family toolbox.

   The inventions may or may not actually be workable. If they are just pretend inventions, have children write or talk about how they would work. If they are real inventions, encourage children to demonstrate how they work.

   Materials for creating inventions could include rubber bands, empty milk cartons, uncooked pieces of spaghetti and noodles, strips of tape, construction paper, plastic bags, straws, craft sticks, and other miscellaneous items.

   Paper clips, tape, brads, staples, and glue might be provided for fastening pieces of the inventions together.

6. Display a list or collection of "useless things"—things people usually toss in the garbage. Invite children to use their green thinking hats to create useful items from these leftovers. For example, lint could be collected and used to stuff a pillow, an old sock could become a cleaning cloth or a puppet, and a broken cup could be turned into a pencil holder.

7. Hold a class discussion about an important current event. Talk about the facts of the issue (white hat thinking), and then invite children to put on their green hats to come up with some possible solutions to the problem. Consider helping children describe their green hat ideas in a letter to the editor that could be published in a local newspaper.

8. Read aloud a poem or book or display a piece of artwork. Do not share the title of the shared item with children. Instead, invite children to use green hat thinking to generate possible titles. Record these on the chalkboard or on chart paper and discuss them. Then share the actual title of the poem, book, or painting.

9. Arrange children into pairs or small groups. Give each group of children a set of objects that can be sorted into groups in a variety of ways, such as a collection of buttons or colored macaroni. Invite children to put on their green hats to think of different ways to classify the objects according to their attributes. Or challenge children to come up with many different combinations for other math concepts, such as coins that equal twenty-five cents or number sentences that equal ten.

Summary

Remember . . .

The green hat is for creative thinking.

With the green hat, we think of *new ideas, possibilities,* or *alternatives.*

The green hat asks *What ideas do we have?*

THE RED HAT

What do I feel about this?

The red hat is worn to express feelings, emotions, hunches, and intuitions. When you explain the red hat to children, ask them to think about the redness of fire. Think of anger and joy but also of warmth and contentment. The red hat includes both intense and more gentle feelings.

When reporting feelings, the thinker may say, "This is what I feel." Unlike the black and yellow hats, the red hat requires no justification, explanation, or logical support.

The red hat covers the feelings at this moment in time: "This is what I feel right now." It may be that in a few minutes the feelings will be different as a result of further information or a perception change.

Feelings, emotions, hunches, and intuitions are all very real, but they are not based on visible logical deduction. At times it is not even possible to explain a feeling: "I have a strong feeling that your plan will work—but I cannot tell you why."

If we are not permitted to put forward our feelings, we simply disguise them as logic and create a rationalization for them. We are then committed to supporting that rationalization. The red hat helps prevent this kind of deception.

Feelings are an important part of thinking. Outside of mathematics and similar "game systems," most thinking involves feelings. We cannot put feelings to one side and pretend that thinking should always be objective and free of feeling. Used at the right place, feelings decide the value of the thinking for ourselves as individuals or for society as a whole. Used at the wrong point, though, feelings can wreck thinking. Strong feelings at the beginning of the thinking (jealousy, fear, anger) so limit perception that thinking can only be used to support these feelings.

The value of the red hat is that it recognizes feelings, emotions, hunches, and intuitions as a valid part of thinking and at the same time labels them for what they are.

The red hat is discussed in more detail in the following teacher notes. Activities for teaching the red hat begin on page 73.

TEACHER NOTES - Red Hat

The following description is intended to serve as background for teacher reference. Consult it when needed to clarify how the red hat may be used and overused.

Shades of Red Hat Thinking

The spectrum of feelings included under the red hat ranges from emotions to intuitions.

Emotions. Here we have normal emotions such as joy, anger, fear, jealousy, and sorrow. Under the influence of these powerful emotions, our perception selects only what supports the emotion. A jealous person will see reasons for jealousy. An angry person will see reasons for anger.

Feelings. This is a general term and covers a much wider range than emotions. There may be feelings of unease or uncertainty. There may be feelings of anxiety. There may be a feeling of potential or of interest. Aesthetics is a feeling. So is the camaraderie that develops when a group works together. The term *feeling* is so broad that it even covers matters like admiration and respect.

Hunches. A hunch lies somewhere between a feeling and an intuition. It takes the form of a strong feeling or decision in favor of or against something. No valid explanation of this decision is available to the person with the hunch. A hunch is something like the vision of a prophet. The hunch seems very real to the person with the hunch, and he or she feels the need to tell others.

Intuitions. There is a claim that intuition is indeed a logical process but that we are not consciously aware of this process. There may be merit to this claim. Intuition may also be the result of complex experiences in the field. It may not be possible to make conscious all the aspects of this experience.

Intuition is often right, but it can also be disastrously wrong. For example, intuitions about probability are notoriously wrong. How many people have lost money gambling when their intuition tells them they are bound to win on the next throw?

Validation of Feelings

The value of the red hat is that it recognizes emotions, feelings, hunches, and intuitions as a valid part of thinking, provided they are signaled as what they are. We can accept an intuition if it is offered as an intuition and not as a logical deduction. We can accept a feeling if it is put forward as such.

The value of the red hat is that it recognizes emotions, feelings, hunches, and intuitions as a valid part of thinking.

Because the device of the red hat makes feelings legitimate, there is no need to apologize for the fact that it is *only* a feeling. Nor—and this is important—is there ever any need to explain or rationalize the feeling. The feeling or intuition now has a validity in its own right: "In spite of all that argument and black hat thinking, I still like the idea."

Focus

Feelings can be focused. A thinker can express a feeling about the total situation or only one part of it: "I like your agenda for the planning session, but I am not happy about having it on May 5."

A thinker may have positive feelings about one aspect of the situa-tion and negative feelings about another. Both these can be put forward provided the focus is given.

Range

It is possible to express a wide range of feelings that vary from the crude to the very subtle. We can like or dislike an idea. We might find an idea attractive or appealing or we might find an idea unattractive or unappealing. We can be happy with an idea or unhappy.

There is also a range of feelings which express unease, uncertainty, and disquiet. These are not as strong as disliking an idea, but we are moving in that direction. We need to be reassured.

We may find an idea boring. This is not to say that it is a bad idea or that it will not work—but just that we do find it boring. It is important with the red hat to realize that feelings must always be subjective. The idea itself is not boring, but *we* find it boring.

The opposite of boring is exciting, interesting, or stimulating. These feelings imply that the idea has potential. It is not just the present form of the idea that is being considered, but all the possibilities opened up by the idea. The idea may not be workable in its present form, but it can still be interesting.

In the end we can probably narrow all these different feelings down to four:

"I like the idea."

"I don't like the idea."

"I am uncertain about the idea."

"I find the idea interesting."

Mixed Feelings

It is legitimate for us to say that we have mixed feelings if this is the case. However, to say that we have mixed feelings as a way of avoiding making our feelings public is not

TEACHER NOTES · Red Hat

legitimate. Most listeners will recognize the escape. In some circles the term *mixed feelings* very clearly indicates that the speaker does not like the idea at all and is politely expressing disapproval.

At times we simply may have no feelings about a matter. If so, we can just report that we do not have any red hat thinking to offer.

Uses of the Red Hat

There are two main uses of the red hat:

1. Making feelings known

2. Making assessments and choices

Making Feelings Known

At any moment we may signal that we are putting on the red hat: "Putting on my red hat, I am unhappy about the demands the community is placing on our schools."

We could have put forward the same feelings without the red hat. It is precisely the formality of labeling the feelings with the red hat, however, that makes the feelings more acceptable.

If there are likely to be strong existing feelings about a matter, then it is helpful to begin discussion of the matter with the red hat. Someone may ask for three minutes of red hat thinking all around. This way background feelings are brought quickly out into the open.

What happens if someone is dishonest about his or her feelings? There is no objective way of checking on feelings. The listener or listeners may, however, express doubt: "I doubt whether those are your true feelings."

Very occasionally we may be permitted to wear the red hat on behalf of someone else. This means that we spell out what we believe the other person's feelings to be: "I am going to put on the red hat for you and to stand in your shoes. I don't think I would like this proposal at all."

On the other hand, if we are just reporting feelings previously expressed by others, that is not red hat but white hat thinking: "Travis told me he is worried about his test scores."

The red hat label can be useful in helping people become aware of what they are doing and insisting that they change their behavior: "That is your red hat thinking—now can you switch to some other hat?" Keep in mind, however, that the red hat is not intended to be just accusatory, but also exploratory: "What are our red hat feelings about this suggestion?"

In general the red hat must be seen as an *opportunity* to make feelings and intuitions known and not a *demand* that these be shared.

Making Assessments and Choices

Before we put any idea into action, we have to use the black hat to be sure we are not making a mistake. The black hat checks out the idea. After this black hat thinking, we then use the red hat: "What do I now feel about the idea?" If the black hat shows that the idea is dangerous or unworkable, we would normally begin to dislike the idea.

There are times, however, when the black hat shows that an idea is dangerous or unworkable, but we like it anyway. In such cases, instead of dismissing the idea completely, we may set out to make the idea more workable. Or we may decide to accept the risks.

In choices or decisions, there is an assessment of each alternative with both yellow and black hats. When this has been done and when the full picture is available, then it is up to the red hat to make the final choice. Which alternative do we *like* best?

In practice we may want to recheck with the black hat: "This is the alternative I like—let me check to see whether anything terrible would happen if I went ahead."

Overuse

There is overuse of the red hat when we use only red hat thinking on all occasions and never do any other sort of thinking.

There is overuse of the red hat when we take up a red hat position and then refuse to look at the information or listen to arguments.

The most common overuse is when we use the red hat too frequently in the course of a discussion. The main value of the red hat is at the beginning (to make feelings known) and at the end (assessment and choice). Frequent red hat interruptions can interfere with the thinking process. Any feelings which have not changed during the course of a discussion can be put forward at the end. There is no point at all in reacting to every comment and suggestion with immediate red hat response.

Summary of the Red Hat

Some key words to describe red hat thinking are *emotions, feelings, hunches,* and *intuition.* The two main uses of the red hat are to disclose feelings and to make assessments and choices. The overall question to ask is *What do I feel about this?*

F ollow these steps to introduce the red hat: lead-in, explanation, and practice.

Lead-in

Help children review the black, yellow, white, and green hats. By now they will know that you are about to introduce another hat, and they may be eager to guess which one is next. Nevertheless, do not acknowledge the color of the fifth hat until after the lead-in.

Focus children on the nature of feelings and emotions by asking some of the following questions.

The Red Hat

"What could I say that might make each of you feel happy?" (You have won a prize, today we will have recess all day long, tomorrow you're going to Disneyland, etc.)

"What could I say that might make each of you feel unhappy?" (The cafeteria has run out of chocolate ice cream, the school carnival has been canceled because of the rain, all of the television stations have gone off the air, etc.)

"What we are talking about are feelings and emotions. Give me some other examples of feelings that people can have." (They might feel happy, sad, jealous, frightened, angry, hungry, curious, etc. Accept all suggestions that could be considered a feeling in the broad sense. See teacher notes, page 71, for more examples.)

"Sometimes we have a feeling that something is true, even though we can't prove that it is. We might have a *hunch* that it's going to rain. Or we might have a *feeling* that our team will win the next ball game.

"What are some hunches that you have had?" (That something good or bad would happen, that school would serve a certain food for lunch, that someone would say or do something that you expected, etc.)

You may want to record children's responses on a large sheet of chart paper using a red marker, or on a large sheet of red paper using a dark marker. Post this response record in the room with the other thinking charts from previous hat discussions.

Explanation

After the lead-in, ask children which hat they have been using. When the red hat has been identified, point out that red hat thinking tells feelings. Mention that red is the color of fire and invite children to share their experiences with fire. Have they ever seen a fire that was big and scary and destroyed property or wildlife? Have they ever been around a cozy campfire which provided warmth and comfort? Red hat thinking is a lot like fire—sometimes roaring hot, sometimes cozy and gentle, and often somewhere in between.

As you model the use of the red hat, withhold explanations about the reasons for your feelings. The red hat is designed to permit the full expression of feeling without defense or apology. Just report how you feel, not why.

"My red hat feeling about the fly in my peanut butter sandwich is *gross!*"

"I will give you my red hat thoughts about the way we sang that song just now. I liked it very much, and I felt very proud of us."

Note: Sometimes people are tempted to misuse the red hat as a means of attacking others. The red hat does not give people permission to be offensive or insulting. "I feel angry" is red hat thinking, but "I feel that you are an idiot" is not. We do not use the red hat to accuse others.

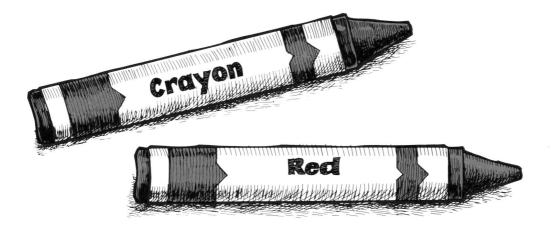

Practice

After the lead-in or on another day, have children work individually to complete the following **Put On Your Red Thinking Hat** reproducible. Read the description and directions aloud. Then invite children to put on their red thinking hats to record their feelings on the chart.

Encourage children to record their answers with a red crayon or a red pen. They may want to compare their answers when everyone has had a chance to complete the page. Create a picture chart or a bar graph of the results for a follow-up math activity.

Consider having children wear red paper hats or visors as you discuss this thinking hat. Hat patterns are provided on pages 102 and 103.

Put On Your Red Thinking Hat

Item	Like	Do Not Like	No Feeling
1. books			
2. bicycles			
3. dogs			
4. summer			
5. snakes			
6. swimming			
7. monsters			
8. broccoli			
9. thunder and lightning			
10. bare feet			
11.			
12.			
13.			
14.			

Edward de Bono / Six Thinking Hats for Schools / K-2 Resource Book
Copyright 1991. McQuaig Group / Published by Perfection Learning Corporation

Put On Your Red Thinking Hat - Teacher Page

Invite children to compare the feelings that they indicated on their handouts. Explain that feelings can vary widely and that all feelings are acceptable. Also establish that feelings do not have to be explained or justified.

Reassure children, too, that feelings can change from moment to moment. Encourage children to feel free to report any changes in their feelings as discussions unfold.

Put On Your Red Thinking Hat

Directions

Use your red hat to think about each of the things on this list.

Then tell your feelings about each thing on the list.

Put a check mark next to each choice to show if you like it, don't like it, or have no feeling about it.

There are four blank spaces on the chart where you may list your own items and record the way you feel about them.

Item	Like	Do Not Like	No Feeling
1. books			
2. bicycles			
3. dogs			
4. summer			
5. snakes			
6. swimming			
7. monsters		*(Answers will vary.)*	
8. broccoli			
9. thunder and lightning			
10. bare feet			
11.			
12.			
13.			
14.			

76

Additional Practice Activities

After introducing the red hat, try the following suggestions for integrating the red hat into other lessons throughout the week. These are only guidelines. Modify or add to them to make the activities relevant and interesting for the children in your classroom. Remember to keep reviewing previous hats too.

1. Return the self-portrait pages children made during the white hat week (see pages 55 and 56, activity 7). Invite each child to add three red hat comments to the information already included on the page. Sample red hat comments are listed below.

    I like/do not like . . .

    I feel scared when . . .

    I felt proud when . . .

    I feel angry when . . .

2. Create a picture file by gluing pictures from magazines and other sources onto index cards or some other sturdy paper. Have children select partners, and distribute several cards to each pair of children.

    Invite one partner to arrange the picture cards into groups according to things they like, things they don't like, and things that they don't have feelings about. Then have the other child in the pair try to guess which label his or her friend gave to each group of pictures. Give each group a new set of cards and repeat the activity, allowing the partners to switch roles this time.

3. Have children keep a red hat reading record for this week. Offer each child a copy of the reproducible provided on the facing page. Encourage children to use red crayons or markers to record their feelings about the books they read or have read to them.

My Red Hat Reading Record

Date	Title	Author	Illustrator	Like	Do Not Like	No Feeling

Edward de Bono / Six Thinking Hats for Schools / K-2 Resource Book
Copyright 1991. McQuaig Group / Published by Perfection Learning Corporation

4. Read aloud a story in which one or more of the characters displays red hat thinking (feelings). As you share the book, discuss with children the examples of red hat thinking in the story. Some suggested titles are listed below.

- *Feelings* by Aliki (Greenwillow, 1984).

- *Sylvester and the Magic Pebble* by William Steig (Windmill, 1969).

- *The Temper Tantrum Book* by Edna Mitchell Preston (Viking, 1969).

- *Things I Like* by Anthony Browne (Knopf, 1989).

5. Read aloud the beginning of a story and invite children to share their red hat thinking (hunches) about what will happen next. Stop two or three times for comments. Some suggested titles are listed below.

- *Alexander and the Terrible, Horrible, No Good, Very Bad Day* by Judith Viorst (Atheneum, 1972).

- *Bedtime for Frances* by Russell Hoban (Harper and Row, 1960).

- *Blueberries for Sal* by Robert McCloskey (Viking, 1948).

- *Lon Po Po: A Red Riding Hood Story from China* by Ed Young (Philomel, 1989).

- *The Paperbag Princess* by Robert Munsch (Annick, 1980).

6. Play a variety of musical selections for the class and encourage children to share the feelings they have that are inspired by the music. Or have children sing or bring in recordings of songs that make them happy, sad, excited, proud, and so forth. This can also be done with art. Display a painting, such as Leonardo da Vinci's *Mona Lisa,* and invite children to share their red hat thinking about the piece.

7. Encourage each child to choose one of the four seasons. Have children wear their red hats to tell what they like and don't like about the seasons they have chosen. Invite interested children to create poems and accompanying illustrations using their red hat ideas.

8. Display pictures of water in different forms and environments, such as water coming out of a faucet, water in a bathtub, water in a pond or large river, floodwater sweeping through a town, and a waterfall. Invite children to put on their red hats and describe their feelings about water in each of the situations shown on the pictures.

Summary

Remember . . .

The red hat is for expressing feelings and hunches.

The red hat requires no justification.

With the red hat, we ask *What do I feel about this?*

The blue hat is different from all of the other hats. The other hats are concerned with thinking about a particular problem or subject. The blue hat is for thinking about the thinking that is being used.

Ask children to imagine the blue sky, which is above everything. If we were up in the sky, we could look down and see what is happening on the ground below. When we use the blue hat, we try to look at the whole view of what we are doing, from the beginning to the end.

We use the blue hat when we are thinking about how to organize what is going on. The blue hat is like the conductor of the orchestra who organizes what instruments are playing at any moment.

At the beginning of a task, the blue hat is used to define the focus and purpose of the task (What are we going to do now?) or to put forward an agenda of steps (What do we need to do first? Then what?). In the middle of a task, the blue hat can be used to make sure the task is on track and that the correct steps are being followed. ("That's a good point, but we were going to talk about trains now," or "What were we going to do after we finished gluing?")

The blue hat is discussed in more detail in the following teacher notes. Activities for teaching the blue hat begin on page 86.

Activities for teaching the blue hat begin on page 86.

THE BLUE HAT

What thinking is needed?

What is the next step?

What thinking has been done?

TEACHER NOTES · Blue Hat

Intelligent people can sometimes be poor thinkers. This is not because they cannot think but because the order in which they carry out their thinking steps is inefficient. It is like having a powerful car but driving it badly. There is nothing wrong with the car but the driver is not making the most of the car's potential.

Consider two thinkers faced with a similar situation. Here is the process each uses to manage the thinking:

Thinker A:

1. This is what I think about this matter.

2. Now I am going to prove to you that I am right.

Thinker B:

1. I want to explore the matter.

2. Here are some alternative views that are possible.

3. This is the view I prefer.

4. Now let me explain how I reached that conclusion.

With Thinker A, the conclusion comes first, and the thinking is just a defense of that conclusion. With Thinker B, there is an exploration of the subject leading to a conclusion which is then explained.

With the blue hat, we can learn to think about our thinking and to plan for better results.

Uses of the Blue Hat

The blue hat is most often used at the beginning, in the middle, and at the end of a thinking session. The five main uses include

1. Defining focus and purpose

2. Setting out a thinking plan or agenda

3. Making observations and comments

4. Deciding the next step

5. Defining outcomes and summarizing

Defining Focus and Purpose

"What are we thinking about?"

"What are we trying to do?"

"What is the desired outcome?"

If we are going somewhere, it is useful to know where we are trying to go. So the blue hat has a very important role to play at the beginning of the thinking.

The blue hat defines the problem or task and the purpose of the thinking. The blue hat lays out the situation.

If we are going somewhere, it is useful to know where we are trying to go. The blue hat defines the problem or task and the purpose of the thinking. The blue hat lays out the situation.

This initial definition of the thinking task need not be done by a single person. The group can discuss the definition with all members of the group wearing blue hats. It is usually helpful to try out several alternative definitions of the task or problem.

The thinking of a group may stray from the purpose of the thinking, or the purpose may change as the thinking unfolds. At such times, someone can put on the blue hat to restate or to redefine what the group is trying to do.

Restating means simply repeating the original thinking task to keep the thinkers on track: "May I put on my blue hat to remind you that we are trying to think of all the creatures that might live in or near a pond."

Redefining indicates a change in the task: "Putting on my blue hat, I would like to note that we have decided to stop thinking about where to have the class picnic until Julie checks on our transportation. Right now we are going to think instead about what food we would like to serve."

Setting Out a Thinking Plan or Agenda

Another blue hat function is to set out an agenda of thinking steps which are to be followed one after the other. An agenda of *subjects* is common enough at meetings. So the idea of an agenda of thinking steps is not a difficult transition.

A simple agenda might be a plan for using the thinking hats in a particular sequence. But a thinking agenda is by no means confined to the use of the six thinking hats. It may cover any thinking process whatsoever.

Making Observations and Comments

Once thinking has begun, we may put on the blue hat to stand back from the thinking in order to comment upon it. The comment may be upon the thinking of another person, the group, or the thinker's own thinking.

"Putting on my blue hat, I feel that we have just been telling what is wrong with this idea, and we should now think about how to improve it."

"My blue hat thinking is that we are trying to think about two

TEACHER NOTES · Blue Hat

different things at once. Let's take one at a time.''

''I'm putting on my blue hat to say that we have just had a great deal of red hat thinking.''

The purpose of a blue hat comment is to be constructive. If we know what we are doing wrong, then we can try to put it right. It may be that the thinking has just concentrated on one part of a problem. It may be that the class has gotten bogged down in an argument between two people. The blue hat provides a mirror in which the thinkers can see their own thinking.

Deciding the Next Step

''What shall we do next?''

''What is the next step?''

It is surprising how much thinking just drifts on from one point to another. What someone says triggers an idea in someone else's mind and that in turn leads to another comment. So it continues. As long as there is no silence or gap, then everyone believes that useful thinking is being done.

The blue hat can stop this drift by making the ''next step'' a conscious decision. The blue hat can be used to propose a next thinking step that can be taken because it is useful—not just because it follows from random conversation.

''Putting on my blue hat, I feel we must have some white hat thinking here.''

''My blue hat thinking is that we list our alternatives first, and then examine each one of them.''

The next step may involve the use of one of the hats, but it can involve any other thinking step at all. It could even include making a decision to *stop* thinking for a while and take a break.

Defining Outcomes and Summarizing

''What conclusion have we reached?''

''What is the outcome?''

At the end of the thinking, we can use the blue hat to insist on an outcome. This outcome can take the form of a solution, conclusion, choice or decision, design, plan, or something else definite—like a promise or a contract.

Where the outcome is not so definite, then the blue hat tries to assess what has been achieved. Perhaps the thinkers have defined a new problem or discovered an obstacle that needs to be confronted. Or the need for some vital information has been identified. Perhaps what has been achieved is a better understanding of the matter. Or possible alternatives have been generated—even if no choice was made.

There is always an outcome of some sort, even if it is not the exact one we sought. In the end, the blue hat seeks to define this outcome, whatever it may be.

The blue hat can also be used to ask for a summary at any stage in the thinking.

''I would like to put on my blue hat and to see what we have done so far. It seems to me that we have made three decisions.''

The thinker can offer his or her own summary or can ask someone else for a summary:

''What have we got so far?''

''Where are we now?''

This request for a summary may also serve to show that very little has been achieved. The summary can then identify problems, obstacles, and information gaps.

Purposes for Using the Blue Hat

The blue hat is usually put on by the person who is suggesting its use. Unlike the other hats, we rarely ask someone else to put on a blue hat. It is possible, however, to suggest that the whole group pause and put on a blue hat to examine the thinking that is taking place or that needs to take place.

The blue hat tends to be announced and used less frequently than the other hats. People often carry out blue hat functions without feeling a need to say so. But it is worthwhile to get into the habit of using the blue hat deliberately and explicitly in order to make easier the shift to the metacognitive level (thinking about thinking).

Overuse

It is possible to belabor thinking by requiring a detailed agenda for every minor task. It is possible to make so many blue hat interruptions during a thinking task that the main purpose of the thinking is forgotten. It is possible to wear the blue hat to ''correct'' people and to tell them that they are doing something wrong. All of these are overuses of the blue hat.

Summary of the Blue Hat

The blue hat is most often used at the beginning, in the middle, and at the end of a thinking session. Some key words to describe the uses of the blue hat are *focus, purpose, agenda, observations, next step, outcome,* and *summary.* Three questions to ask with the blue hat are *What thinking is needed?, What is the next step?,* and *What thinking has been done?*

Follow these steps to introduce the blue hat: lead-in, explanation, and practice.

Lead-in

Help children review the other hats. Tell them that now they are going to learn about the last hat. See if they can remember which hat that will be. Remember, do not acknowledge the color of the sixth hat until after the lead-in.

To introduce the blue hat, choose a simple recipe, such as making peanut butter sandwiches, gelatin, or applesauce. Write the steps for completing the recipe in blue marker on large cards or sheets of chart paper, with one step on each card or page. Mix the cards or chart papers so that the steps are out of order. Display all of the steps and challenge children to reorganize them into a logical, workable order. Then provide the necessary ingredients and help the class follow the recipe to make the treat. As children enjoy the snack, hold a class discussion about what might have happened if the recipe had been followed as it was first presented—with all of the steps mixed up.

Explanation

After the lead-in, ask children which hat they have been using. When the blue hat has been identified, point out that the blue hat is for thinking about thinking. Point out that when the children thought through the recipe first and organized the steps they were going to follow, they were planning in order to reach a goal. Children will be doing blue hat thinking when they organize their thinking to make it more clear, just as they organized the recipe to make it useful.

In a typical classroom setting, blue hat thinking is often done by the teacher. Point out to children when you are wearing your blue hat to keep the discussion on track or to organize an activity. In addition, invite children to help in blue hat thinking by asking questions.

"Who can do some blue hat thinking and help decide the steps we could take to think of a name for our library corner?"

"Who can wear the blue hat and tell us which hat we were using when we were sharing our feelings about the story?"

Practice

After the lead-in or on another day, have children work individually, in small groups, or as a class to complete the following **Put On Your Blue Thinking Hat** reproducible. Read the description and directions aloud. Explain that this activity is a kind of mixed-up recipe for catching a frog. Encourage children to use blue hat thinking to organize the thinking steps for catching a frog.

When children are finished, encourage them to share their responses with the class. Record the thinking steps in the correct order on a large sheet of chart paper using a blue marker or on a sheet of blue paper using a dark marker. Post this sheet in the room with the other hat response charts.

Consider having children wear blue paper hats or visors as you discuss this thinking hat. Hat patterns are provided on pages 102 and 103.

Put On Your Blue Thinking Hat

You see a frog and you want to catch it.

Look at the thinking steps at the bottom of the page.

Which would you think about first, second, and last?

Cut out the steps. Put them on the Thinking Map in order.

Pick one plan and try it.

Think about what you did. Did your plan work? Did you catch the frog?

Think of ways to catch a frog.

Edward de Bono / Six Thinking Hats for Schools / K-2 Resource Book
Copyright 1991. McQuaig Group / Published by Perfection Learning Corporation

How to Catch a Frog Thinking Map

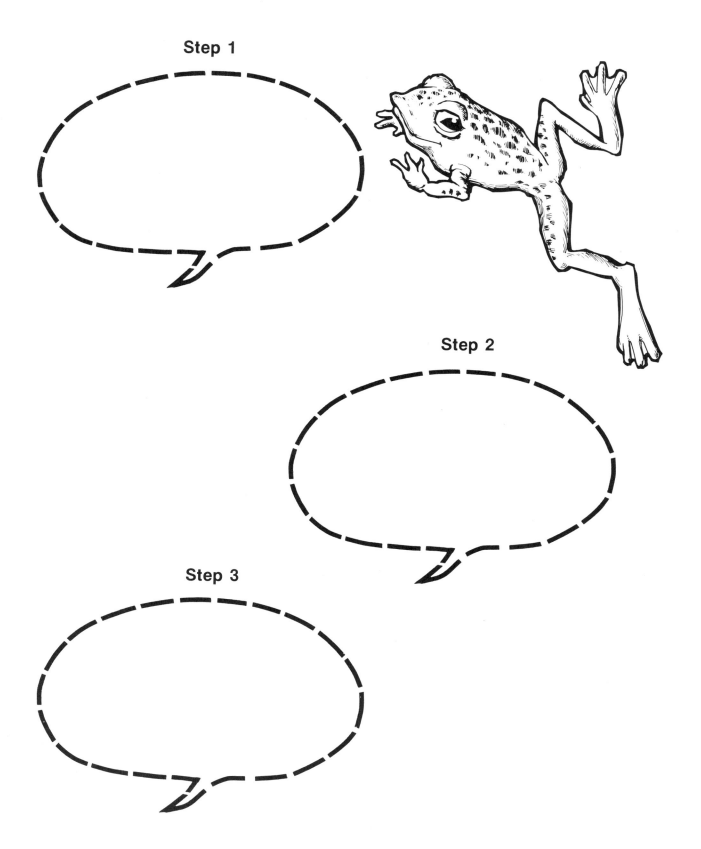

Step 1

Step 2

Step 3

Edward de Bono / Six Thinking Hats for Schools / K-2 Resource Book
Copyright 1991. McQuaig Group / Published by Perfection Learning Corporation

Put On Your Blue Thinking Hat - Teacher Page

Ask children to compare their papers and find out whether everyone placed the steps in the same order. Invite some children to explain how they designed their thinking plans. The example at right shows a likely response. However, someone may be able to justify an alternative.

During the discussion, focus the children's comments on the order of the thinking steps. Guide children away from lengthy discussions about various methods of catching frogs.

How to Catch a Frog Thinking Map

Step 1

Think of ways to catch a frog.

Step 2

Pick one plan and try it.

Step 3

Think about what you did. Did your plan work? Did you catch the frog?

89

Additional Practice Activities

After introducing the blue hat, try the following suggestions for integrating the blue hat into other lessons throughout the week. These are only guidelines. Modify or add to them to make the activities relevant and interesting for the children in your classroom.

1. Ask children to put on their blue hats and help you think about how to draw a picture of the school building on the chalkboard or overhead projector. Encourage them to tell you where you should begin, what should be included in the picture, and so forth. Collect several responses before you begin to draw. Then show how you are using the comments to avoid difficulties.

   "Lonnie said we should draw the sidewalk. Let's put it way down here so there will be lots of room left to draw the building."

   After you draw the school building, offer each child paper and pencils, crayons, or markers. Invite children to draw pictures of the houses or buildings where they live. Encourage them to put on their blue hats and plan the drawing before they begin, just as you did in drawing the school picture.

2. After a field trip or another special activity, encourage children to use blue hat thinking to plan a newsletter to report on the event. For example, children may decide to write all of the white hat facts about the trip first, then record their black and yellow hat observations, and then list green hat suggestions for changing or improving their next field trip. The newsletter could be decorated with red hat faces to show how children felt about the event. Planning and writing the newsletter could be done individually, in small groups, or as a whole class project.

3. Before children begin working on an assignment, such as a math problem or a science experiment, ask them to read the directions and then restate in their own words what they are supposed to do. This will help children practice the blue hat functions of defining purpose and summarizing outcomes.

4. Encourage children to keep thinking journals for at least one week. Invite children to record the different kinds of thinking they do during the week. For example, you may request that each child list two examples of green hat thinking they did on Monday, two white hat examples for Tuesday, and so on. Or let children do the blue hat thinking to create a plan for organizing their own journals. In either case, children will begin to think about their thinking, which is the main function of the blue hat. For beginning writers, you may want to provide sentence starters such as the following.

> I thought about what might go wrong when . . .
> (black hat)
>
> I thought about the good points of . . .
> (yellow hat)
>
> I felt . . .
> (red hat)
>
> I thought about facts when . . .
> (white hat)
>
> I thought new and different ideas when . . .
> (green hat)
>
> I thought about what order to do things in when . . .
> (blue hat)

Invite interested children to share some of their entries with a partner or the whole class during a group discussion.

5. Help children use the six thinking hats to organize a cooperative class project. This could include a field trip, a service project for the school or community, or a class party. For example, after children have learned all of the six thinking hats, they may want to celebrate their new thinking skills by planning a thinking hats party. Help children use the six thinking hats to plan, host, and evaluate the party. A sample sequence of events is shown below.

Blue Hat: Think about what will have to be done first, second, third, and so on, to plan the party

Green Hat: Think of possibilities for time, place, refreshments, and games

Yellow Hat: Discuss the good points of each green hat possibility

Black Hat: Think about the bad points of each green hat possibility

Red Hat: Share feelings about each green hat possibility

White Hat: List who will be responsible for providing refreshments, supplies for games, arranging facilities, sending invitations, and so on

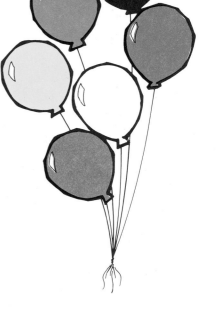

HAVE THE PARTY!!

Red Hat: Share feelings about the party

Yellow Hat: Discuss the good points of the party

Black Hat: Discuss the bad points and weaknesses of the party

Green Hat: Discuss ways of improving the next class party

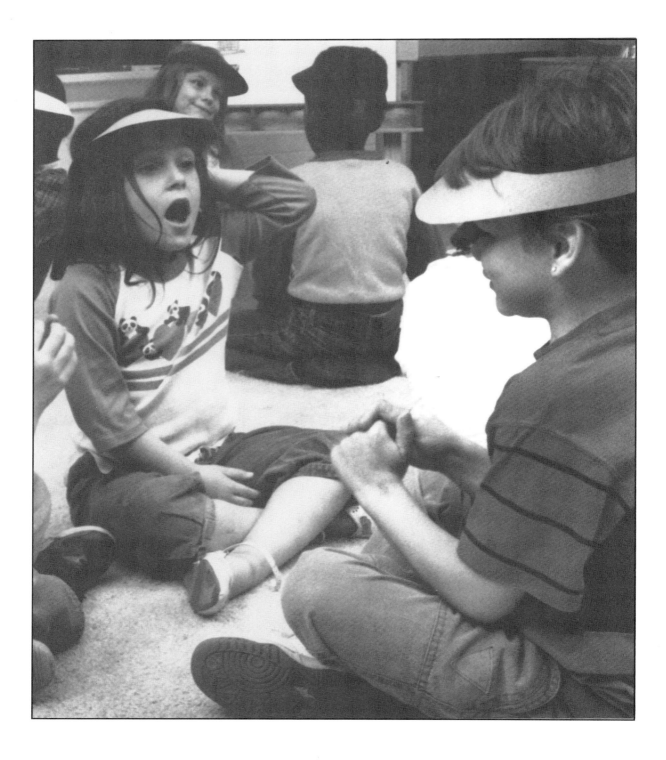

Summary

Remember . . .

Wearing the blue hat is like being in the sky above, looking down at a situation and planning for the best way to think about it.

The blue hat has two functions: to look at the thinking that we are doing and to tell us what thinking to do next.

The blue hat asks *What thinking is needed?*
What is the next step? and
What thinking has been done?

MY THINKING PLAN

The blank thinking plan reproducible provided on the following page can be used to help children plan a variety of thinking tasks. You can choose to have children develop their own thinking plan or have them work from a thinking structure that you have created.

Along with class projects, the thinking plan reproducible can be used by children individually or in small groups as they become more familiar with the hats and their roles.

My Thinking Plan

Project: _____

FINAL WORD

I shall list here a summary of what I consider to be the yellow hat points about the six hat method.

1. The method provides a colorful and fun way of paying attention to thinking. Thinking is usually abstract and boring.

2. The colors and the hats provide a useful mental image that is easy to learn and easy to remember.

3. The six hat method may be used at the simplest possible level but may also be used at a sophisticated level. It has already been in use with six-year-olds and with senior executives in the world's largest businesses.

4. The hats provide a framework for organizing thinking so that it is no longer a matter of drift and argument. Thinking becomes more focused, more constructive, and more productive.

5. In a family, community, school, or organization, once the hats have been learned they become a sort of language for discussing thinking.

6. The hats avoid confusion by allowing a thinker to do just one thing at a time and to do that well.

7. The hats provide a thinking step to do next. They can also provide an overall agenda or framework to guide thinking.

8. The hats can be used to request a certain type of thinking or to request a change from a type of thinking. Taken together this can mean a request for a *switch* in thinking.

9. Because of their artificiality, the hats can be used to ask for a change in thinking without giving offense.

10. The game and role-playing nature of the hats allows for the detachment of the ego from the thinking: "This is not me, but my red hat thinking." This is most important for good thinking.

11. The hats acknowledge that emotions, feelings, and intuition are an important part of practical thinking. The hats allow feelings to come into thinking at the most useful time instead of coming in at the most destructive time.

12. The hats allow full attention to be paid to the critical aspects of thinking (black hat), the constructive aspects of thinking (yellow hat), and the creative aspects of thinking (green hat). Thinking is too often just critical in nature. The hats show that critical thinking is an important part of thinking—but is just one part.

13. The six hat method is easy to teach and easy to learn.

14. The hats provide a framework for learning about the different aspects of thinking and for understanding thinking. Without them, it can be difficult to teach thinking.

15. The hats provide a method for teaching different habits and operations in thinking. These find their place under the different hats. For example, the habits of critical thinking fit naturally under the black hat.

16. Important aspects of thinking, such as formulating hypotheses, speculating, and identifying possibilities, can be taught in a practical manner (green hat).

17. The blue hat provides a simple way of doing the most difficult thing—thinking about thinking. The ability to stand back and watch and control one's own thinking is essential for good thinking but very difficult to teach. The blue hat makes this metacognition more accessible.

18. The six hats provide a simple and practical method for spreading good thinking habits since the hats can easily be explained to other people.

19. The six hats are so basic that they cut across boundaries of culture and ideology. All hats are important. All hats are of great value.

20. The hats provide a simple and practical way of showing that thinking is a skill that can be learned, practiced, and improved. The hats show that thinking is not just a matter of intelligence, of information, or of arguing.

Six Thinking Hats for Schools
Teacher Resource Books
     Grades K-2
     Grades 3-5
     Grades 6-8
     Grades 9-12
Six Thinking Hats Wall Chart
Six Thinking Hats Journal
Six Thinking Hats Board Game

Think, Note, Write Student
Workbooks and Teacher Guides
     Green Level (Grade 6), Books 1 and 2
     Blue Level (Grade 7), Books 1 and 2
     Red Level (Grade 8), Books 1 and 2
     Purple Level (Grade 9), Books 1 and 2
Think, Note, Write Reproducible Tool Boxes
Think, Note, Write Posters (set of 18)

Edward de Bono Thinking Skills Programs Published by Perfection Learning

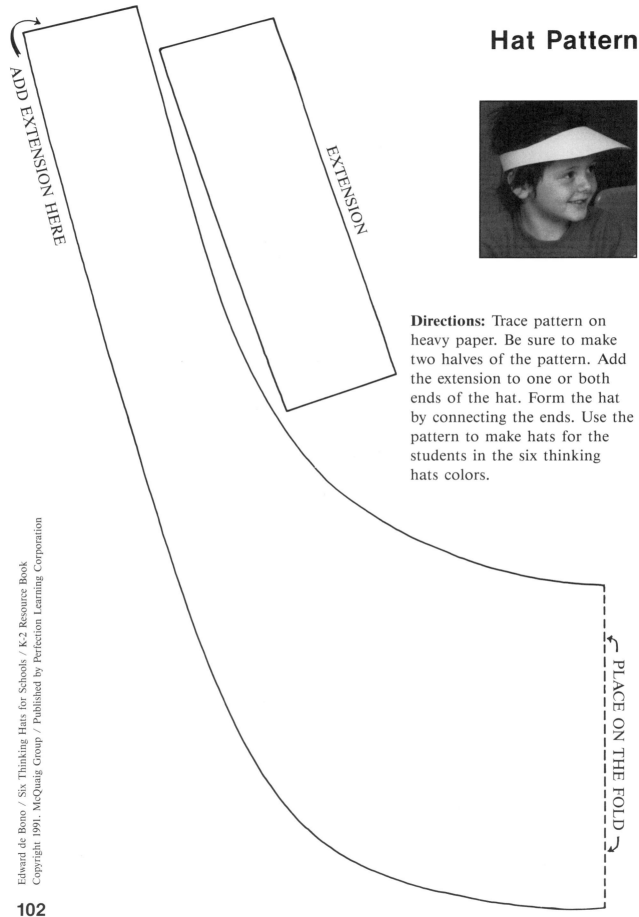

Hat Pattern

Directions: Trace pattern on heavy paper. Be sure to make two halves of the pattern. Add the extension to one or both ends of the hat. Form the hat by connecting the ends. Use the pattern to make hats for the students in the six thinking hats colors.

ADD EXTENSION HERE

EXTENSION

PLACE ON THE FOLD

Hat Pattern

NOTES